CLEVERLili

12

STUDY GUIDE

A Divided Union: Civil Rights in the USA, 1945–74

Edexcel - IGCSE

app available

www.GCSEHistory.com

CLEVER Lili

Published by Clever Lili Limited.

contact@cleverlili.com

First published 2020

ISBN 978-1-913887-11-7

Copyright notice

All rights reserved. No part of this publication may be reproduced in any form or by any means (including photocopying or storing it in any medium by electronic means and whether or not transiently or incidentally to some other use of this publication) with the written permission of the copyright owner. Applications for the copyright owner's written permission should be addressed to the publisher.

Clever Lili has made every effort to contact copyright holders for permission for the use of copyright material. We will be happy, upon notification, to rectify any errors or omissions and include any appropriate rectifications in future editions.

Cover by: Warren K. Leffler / Library of Congress on Unsplash

Icons by: flaticon and freepik

Contributors: Lynn Harkin, Muirin Gillespie-Gallery

Edited by Paul Connolly and Rebecca Parsley

Design by Evgeni Veskov and Will Fox

All rights reserved

DISCOVER MORE OF OUR IGCSE HISTORY STUDY GUIDES
GCSEHistory.com and Clever Lili

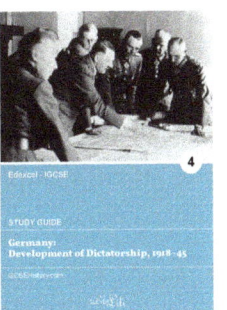

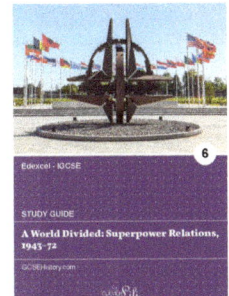

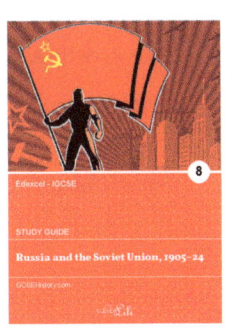

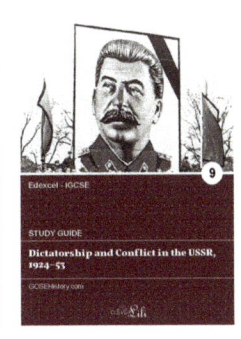

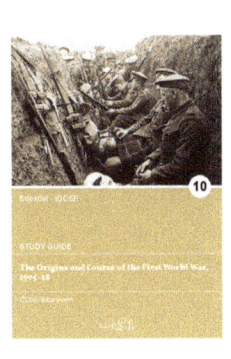

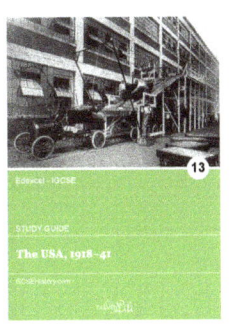

- Edexcel - IGCSE STUDY GUIDE: Germany: Development of Dictatorship, 1918-45
- Edexcel - IGCSE STUDY GUIDE: A World Divided: Superpower Relations, 1943-72
- Edexcel - IGCSE STUDY GUIDE: Russia and the Soviet Union, 1905-24
- Edexcel - IGCSE STUDY GUIDE: Dictatorship and Conflict in the USSR, 1924-53
- Edexcel - IGCSE STUDY GUIDE: The Origins and Course of the First World War, 1905-18
- Edexcel - IGCSE STUDY GUIDE: The Vietnam Conflict, 1945-75
- Edexcel - IGCSE STUDY GUIDE: The USA, 1918-41
- Edexcel - IGCSE STUDY GUIDE: Changes in Medicine, c1848-c1948
- Edexcel - IGCSE STUDY GUIDE: China: Conflict, Crisis and Change, 1900-89

THE GUIDES ARE EVEN BETTER WITH OUR GCSE/IGCSE HISTORY WEBSITE APP AND MOBILE APP

GCSE History is a text and voice web and mobile app that allows you to easily revise for your GCSE/IGCSE exams wherever you are - it's like having your own personal GCSE history tutor. Whether you're at home or on the bus, GCSE History provides you with thousands of convenient bite-sized facts to help you pass your exams with flying colours. We cover all topics - with more than 120,000 questions - across the Edexcel, AQA and CIE exam boards.

GCSEHistory.com — GET IT ON Google Play — Download on the App Store

Contents

How to use this book 6
What is this book about? 7
Revision suggestions 9

Timelines
A Divided Union: Civil Rights in the USA, 1945-74 13

The American Political System
The US Government 16
US Political System 18

Causes of the Red Scare
Cold War 18
Satellite States 20
Iron Curtain Speech, 1946 21
Truman Doctrine, 1947 22
Marshall Plan, 1947 23
Berlin Blockade, 1948-49 24
Berlin Airlift, 1948-49 25
Soviet Union Nuclear Weapons 26
Korean War, 1950-53 26

McCarthyism and the Red Scare
Red Scare 29
The 1950s Red Scare 29
Hollywood Ten, 1947 31
Alger Hiss Case, 1948 to 1950 32
Rosenberg Case, 1951 33
McCarthyism 34

Background to Civil Rights in the 1950s
Treatment of Black Americans 35
Segregation 36
Discrimination 37
President Truman and Civil Rights 38
Civil Rights 39
National Association for the Advancement of Colored People ... 39
Congress of Racial Equality 40
Regional Council of Negro Leadership 41
Southern Christian Leadership Council 41
Universities 42
Churches 42

Civil Rights in the 1950s
Brown v Topeka, 1954 43
Emmett Till Murder, 1955 44
Montgomery Bus Boycott, 1955-56 46

Little Rock High School, 1957 48
Bussing 50
Civil Rights Act, 1957 51
Martin Luther King 52

Opposition to Civil Rights
Opposition to Civil Rights 53
Ku Klux Klan 53
Dixiecrats 54

The Impact of Civil Rights Protests, 1960 to 1965
Sit-Ins, 1960 55
Student Nonviolent Coordinating Committee 56
Freedom Riders, 1961 57
James Meredith Case, 1961 59
Campaign C, 1963 59
Washington March, 1963 61
Freedom Summer, 1964 62
Mississippi Murders, 1964 64
Civil Rights Act, 1964 65
Selma, 1964 66
Voting Rights Act, 1965 67

Malcolm X
Malcolm X 68

The Black Power Movement
Black Power 70
Support for Black Power 71
Stokely Carmichael 72
Mexico Olympics, 1968 72
Black Panthers, 1966 73
Race Riots, 1964-67 74
Kerner Report, 1968 76

Civil Rights Movement in the Late 1960s
Campaign in the North, 1968 76
Martin Luther King Assassination, 1968 78
Civil Rights Act, 1968 79
Poor People's Campaign, 1968 79
John F Kennedy 80
John F Kennedy and Civil Rights 81
Lyndon B Johnson 82
Richard Nixon 83

Other Protest Movements
Other Protest Movements 84

Quizzes, amazing exam preparation tools and more at GCSEHistory.com

Student Movement

Student Protest 85

Student Movement 86

Berkeley Free Speech Movement, 1964-65 88

Kent State University Protests, 1970 89

Hippy Movement 90

Vietnam War 91

Opposition to Vietnam War 93

Women's Movement

Women's Movement 95

Eleanor Roosevelt 97

Betty Friedan 98

Phyllis Schlafly 99

Equal Pay Act, 1963 99

National Organisation for Women 100

Equal Rights Amendment, 1972 101

Women's Liberation Movement 101

Abortion 102

Roe v Wade, 1973 102

Nixon and Watergate

Watergate Scandal, 1972 103

Glossary 107

Index 111

HOW TO USE THIS BOOK

In this study guide, you will see a series of icons, highlighted words and page references. The key below will help you quickly establish what these mean and where to go for more information.

Icons

WHAT questions cover the key events and themes.

WHO questions cover the key people involved.

WHEN questions cover the timings of key events.

WHERE questions cover the locations of key moments.

WHY questions cover the reasons behind key events.

HOW questions take a closer look at the way in which events, situations and trends occur.

IMPORTANCE questions take a closer look at the significance of events, situations, and recurrent trends and themes.

DECISIONS questions take a closer look at choices made at events and situations during this era.

Highlighted words

Abdicate - occasionally, you will see certain words highlighted within an answer. This means that, if you need it, you'll find an explanation of the word or phrase in the glossary which starts on **page 107**.

Page references

Tudor *(p.7)* - occasionally, a certain subject within an answer is covered in more depth on a different page. If you'd like to learn more about it, you can go directly to the page indicated.

WHAT IS THIS BOOK ABOUT?

A divided union: civil rights in the USA, 1945-74 is the period study investigating the issues that divided America, how these issues were challenged, and to what extent the challenges were successful. You will focus on crucial events during this period, and study the different political, economic and social changes that occurred.

Purpose
This study will help you understand the complexities of America between 1945 and 1974. You will investigate themes such as communism, capitalism, racism, segregation, discrimination, sexism, counter-culture, equal rights, boycotts and protest. This course enables you to develop the historical skills of identifying key features of a time period, and encourages you to analyse and compare sources and evaluate interpretations.

Topics
A divided union: civil rights in the USA, 1945-74 is split into 5 enquiries:

- Enquiry 1 looks at the Red Scare and McCarthyism. You will investigate the reasons why the USA was gripped by the Red Scare and the key events that took place during it, including the Hiss and Rosenberg trials. You will study the impact of the Red Scare on America.
- Enquiry 2 looks at civil rights in the 1950s. You will investigate the issues of segregation and discrimination. You will study the impact of early civil rights cases such as Brown v Topeka and the murder of Emmett Till, as well as the significance of key civil rights protests and the impact of the KKK.
- Enquiry 3 looks at the impact of civil rights protests between 1960 and 1974. You will study the significance and impact of the Freedom Riders and sit-ins, as well as the role of individuals and organisations on the development of the civil rights movement from Martin Luther King to the Black Power movement.
- Enquiry 4 looks at other protest movements that developed because of the Vietnam War and counterculture movement such as the hippies. You will also study the women's movement and the reasons why there was opposition to it.
- Enquiry 5 looks at President Nixon and the Watergate scandal. You will investigate the causes of the scandal, what happened and the impact it had on American politics.

Key Individuals
Some of the key individuals studied on this course include:

- Senator McCarthy.
- Ethel and Julius Rosenberg.
- Emmett Till.
- President Kennedy.
- President Johnson.
- Martin Luther King Jr.
- Malcolm X.
- President Nixon.

Key Events
Some of the key events you will study on this course include:

- The Trial of Alger Hiss.
- The Execution of the Rosenbergs.
- The Montgomery Bus Boycott.
- The Civil Rights Act, 1957.
- The Black Panthers.
- Anti-Vietnam and Student Protests.
- The Watergate Scandal.

Assessment
A divided union: civil rights in the USA, 1945-74 forms part of paper 1 which you have a total of 1 hour and 30 minutes to complete. You should spend 45 minutes on this section of the paper. There will be 1 exam question on A divided union: civil rights in the USA, 1945-74. The question will be broken down into 4 sections: a, b, c(i) and c(ii). You will answer a, b and either c(i) or c(ii).

Get our free app at GCSEHistory.com

WHAT IS THIS BOOK ABOUT?

- Question a is worth 6 marks. This question requires you to examine an extract and assesses your ability to analyse and evaluate a historical interpretation. You will need to identify the author's opinion or perspective by analysing the language the author uses and what they have chosen to comment on. You will explain how valid the overall impression is by using your own knowledge to evaluate that impression.

- Question b is worth 8 marks. This question requires you to explain two effects of an event on something else by using your contextual knowledge and looking at the consequences. You will need to identify two effects and then demonstrate how the event led to the effect you have identified.

- Question c(i) and c(ii) are worth 16 marks. This question requires you to construct an argument to support and challenge an interpretation stated in the question. You will be given two pieces of information to help jog your memory but you must use information of your own. You will have the opportunity to show your ability to explain and analyse historical events using second order concepts such as causation, consequence, change, continuity, similarity and difference.

Quizzes, amazing exam preparation tools and more at GCSEHistory.com

REVISION SUGGESTIONS

Revision! A dreaded word. Everyone knows it's coming, everyone knows how much it helps with your exam performance, and everyone struggles to get started! We know you want to do the best you can in your IGCSEs, but schools aren't always clear on the best way to revise. This can leave students wondering:

- ✓ How should I plan my revision time?
- ✓ How can I beat procrastination?
- ✓ What methods should I use? Flash cards? Re-reading my notes? Highlighting?

Luckily, you no longer need to guess at the answers. Education researchers have looked at all the available revision studies, and the jury is in. They've come up with some key pointers on the best ways to revise, as well as some thoughts on popular revision methods that aren't so helpful. The next few pages will help you understand what we know about the best revision methods.

How can I beat procrastination?

This is an age-old question, and it applies to adults as well! Have a look at our top three tips below.

Reward yourself

When we think a task we have to do is going to be boring, hard or uncomfortable, we often put if off and do something more 'fun' instead. But we often don't really enjoy the 'fun' activity because we feel guilty about avoiding what we should be doing. Instead, get your work done and promise yourself a reward after you complete it. Whatever treat you choose will seem all the sweeter, and you'll feel proud for doing something you found difficult. Just do it!

Just do it!

We tend to procrastinate when we think the task we have to do is going to be difficult or dull. The funny thing is, the most uncomfortable part is usually making ourselves sit down and start it in the first place. Once you begin, it's usually not nearly as bad as you anticipated.

Pomodoro technique

The pomodoro technique helps you trick your brain by telling it you only have to focus for a short time. Set a timer for 20 minutes and focus that whole period on your revision. Turn off your phone, clear your desk, and work. At the end of the 20 minutes, you get to take a break for five. Then, do another 20 minutes. You'll usually find your rhythm and it becomes easier to carry on because it's only for a short, defined chunk of time.

Spaced practice

We tend to arrange our revision into big blocks. For example, you might tell yourself: "This week I'll do all my revision for the Cold War, then next week I'll do the Medicine Through Time unit."

Get our free app at GCSEHistory.com

REVISION SUGGESTIONS

This is called **massed practice**, because all revision for a single topic is done as one big mass.

But there's a better way! Try **spaced practice** instead. Instead of putting all revision sessions for one topic into a single block, space them out. See the example below for how it works.

This means planning ahead, rather than leaving revision to the last minute - but the evidence strongly suggests it's worth it. You'll remember much more from your revision if you use **spaced practice** rather than organising it into big blocks. Whichever method you choose, though, remember to reward yourself with breaks.

Spaced practice (more effective):

week 1	week 2	week 3	week 4
Topic 1	Topic 1	Topic 1	Topic 1
Topic 2	Topic 2	Topic 2	Topic 2
Topic 3	Topic 3	Topic 3	Topic 3
Topic 4	Topic 4	Topic 4	Topic 4

Massed practice (less effective)

week 1	week 2	week 3	week 4
Topic 1	Topic 2	Topic 3	Topic 4

REVISION SUGGESTIONS

What methods should I use to revise?

Self-testing/flash cards

Self explanation/mind-mapping

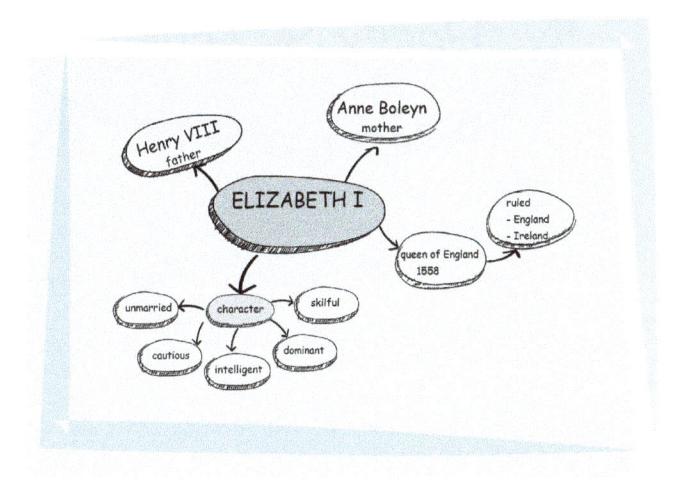

The research shows a clear winner for revision methods - **self-testing**. A good way to do this is with **flash cards**. Flash cards are really useful for helping you recall short – but important – pieces of information, like names and dates.

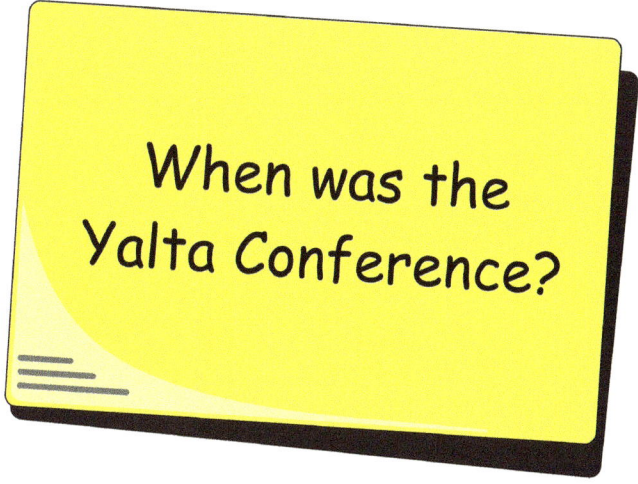

Side A - question

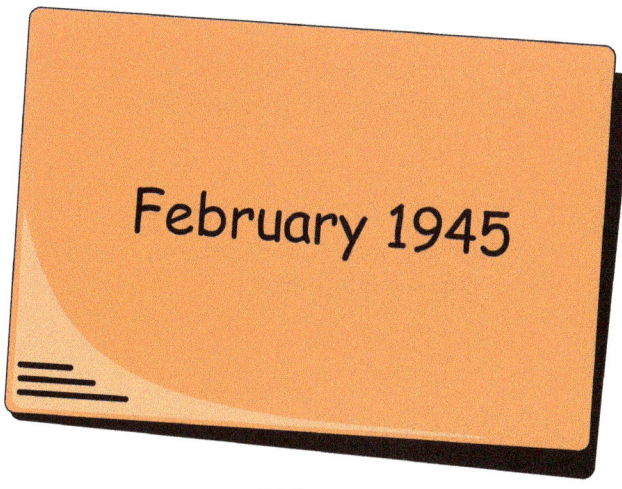

Side B - answer

Write questions on one side of the cards, and the answers on the back. This makes answering the questions and then testing yourself easy. Put all the cards you get right in a pile to one side, and only repeat the test with the ones you got wrong - this will force you to work on your weaker areas.

pile with right answers

pile with wrong answers

As this book has a quiz question structure itself, you can use it for this technique.

Another good revision method is **self-explanation**. This is where you explain how and why one piece of information from your course linked with another piece.

This can be done with **mind-maps**, where you draw the links and then write explanations for how they connect. For example, President Truman is connected with anti-communism because of the Truman Doctrine.

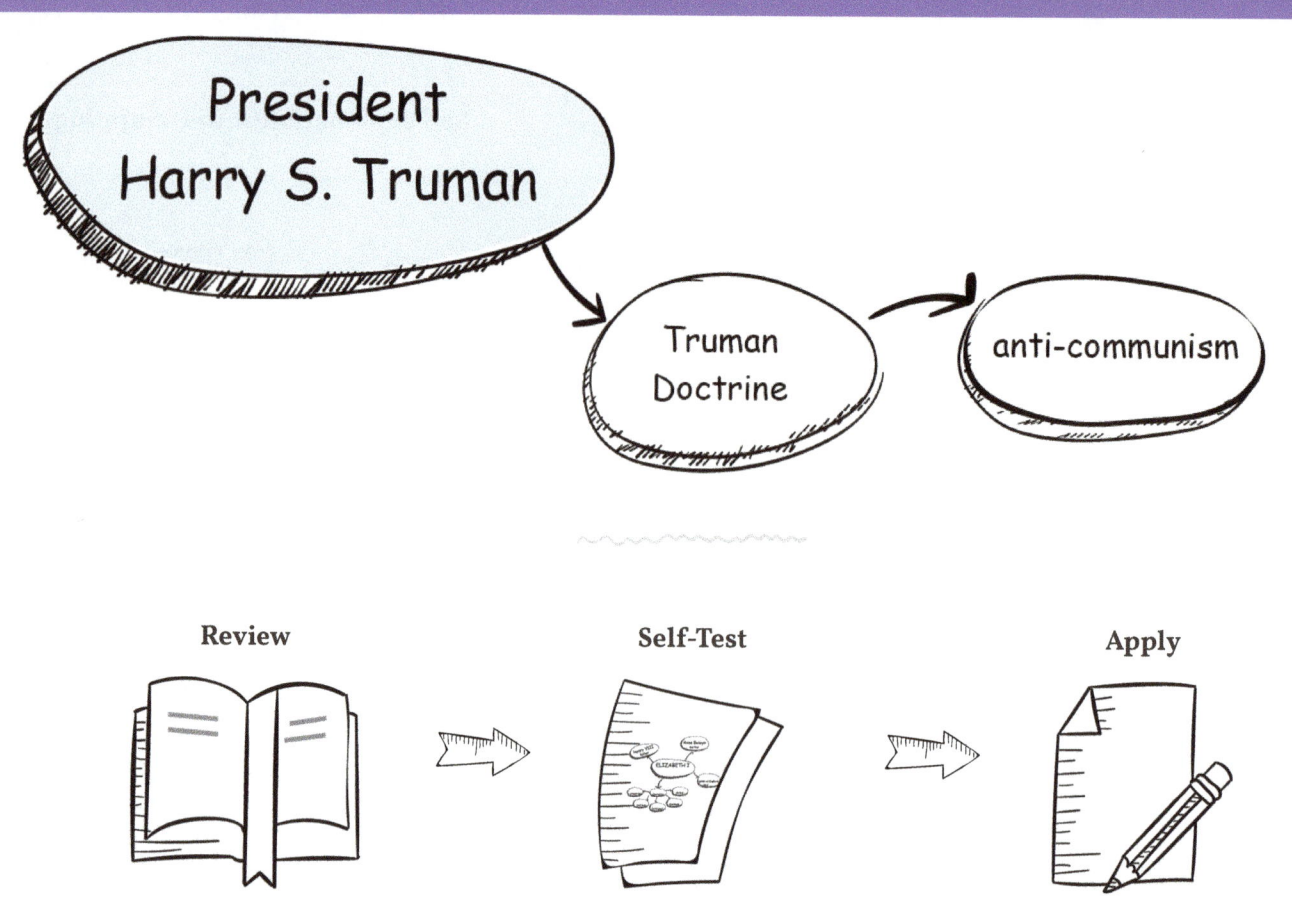

REVISION SUGGESTIONS

President Harry S. Truman → Truman Doctrine → anti-communism

Review
Start by highlighting or re-reading to create your flashcards for self-testing.

Self-Test
Test yourself with flash cards. Make mind maps to explain the concepts.

Apply
Apply your knowledge on practice exam questions.

Which revision techniques should I be cautious about?

Highlighting and **re-reading** are not necessarily bad strategies - but the research does say they're less effective than flash cards and mind-maps.

Highlighting

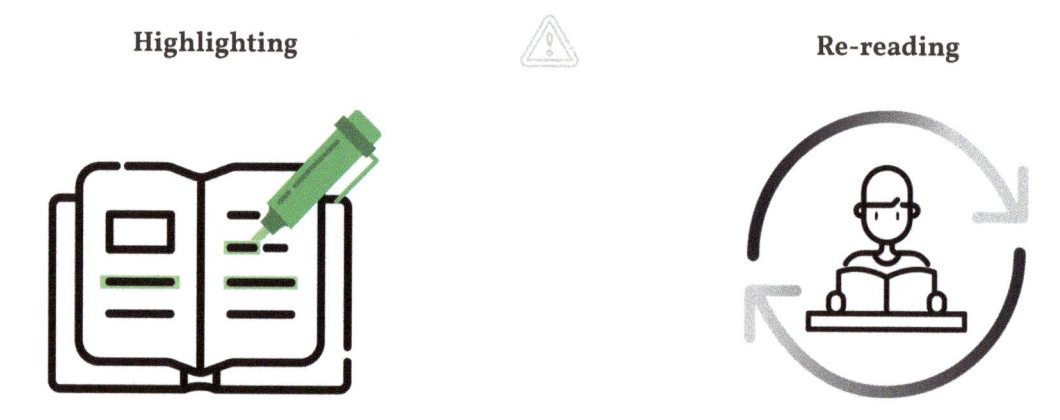

Re-reading

If you do use these methods, make sure they are **the first step to creating flash cards**. Really engage with the material as you go, rather than switching to autopilot.

Quizzes, amazing exam preparation tools and more at GCSEHistory.com

A DIVIDED UNION: CIVIL RIGHTS IN THE USA, 1945-74

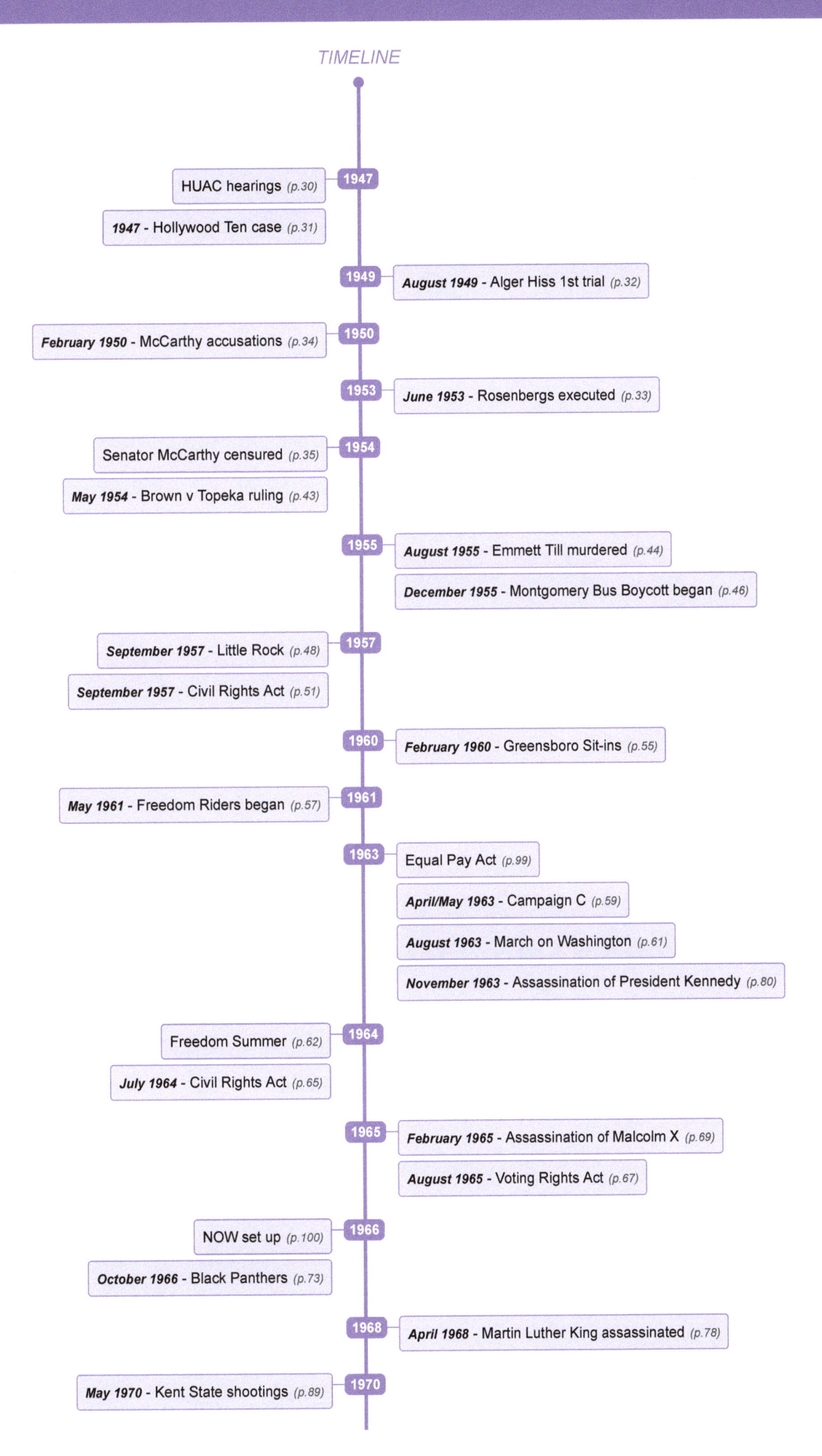

TIMELINE

1947
- HUAC hearings *(p.30)*
- *1947* - Hollywood Ten case *(p.31)*

1949
- *August 1949* - Alger Hiss 1st trial *(p.32)*

1950
- *February 1950* - McCarthy accusations *(p.34)*

1953
- *June 1953* - Rosenbergs executed *(p.33)*

1954
- Senator McCarthy censured *(p.35)*
- *May 1954* - Brown v Topeka ruling *(p.43)*

1955
- *August 1955* - Emmett Till murdered *(p.44)*
- *December 1955* - Montgomery Bus Boycott began *(p.46)*

1957
- *September 1957* - Little Rock *(p.48)*
- *September 1957* - Civil Rights Act *(p.51)*

1960
- *February 1960* - Greensboro Sit-ins *(p.55)*

1961
- *May 1961* - Freedom Riders began *(p.57)*

1963
- Equal Pay Act *(p.99)*
- *April/May 1963* - Campaign C *(p.59)*
- *August 1963* - March on Washington *(p.61)*
- *November 1963* - Assassination of President Kennedy *(p.80)*

1964
- Freedom Summer *(p.62)*
- *July 1964* - Civil Rights Act *(p.65)*

1965
- *February 1965* - Assassination of Malcolm X *(p.69)*
- *August 1965* - Voting Rights Act *(p.67)*

1966
- NOW set up *(p.100)*
- *October 1966* - Black Panthers *(p.73)*

1968
- *April 1968* - Martin Luther King assassinated *(p.78)*

1970
- *May 1970* - Kent State shootings *(p.89)*

Get our free app at GCSEHistory.com

A DIVIDED UNION: CIVIL RIGHTS IN THE USA, 1945-74

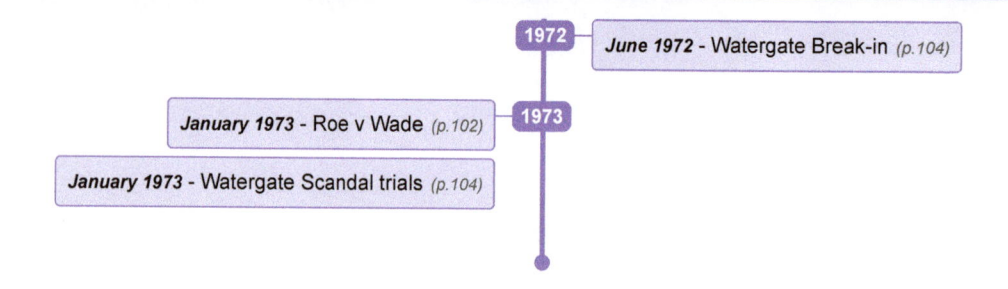

1972
June 1972 - Watergate Break-in *(p.104)*

1973
January 1973 - Roe v Wade *(p.102)*
January 1973 - Watergate Scandal trials *(p.104)*

THE US GOVERNMENT

'To live under the American constitution is the greatest political privilege that was ever accorded to the human race.' - President Calvin Coolidge

How does the American government work?

The USA is a democracy and a republic. Its government is defined by the constitution, which sets out how it should be run.

What role does the constitution play in the American government?

The constitution is a set of laws that define how America is run. It is seen as having the highest authority in any government.

How is the constitution amended in the American government?

The American constitution is designed to be difficult to amend. There are 2 main ways it can be done.

- ☑ Congress has to pass the amendment with a two-thirds majority in both houses. It then has to be approved by three quarters of all state legislatures.
- ☑ A constitutional convention can be called to draft an amendment if desired by two thirds of all states. This method has never been used.

What does unconstitutional mean in the American government?

Anything that breaks the laws of the constitution is said to be unconstitutional and can not legally exist.

What were the powers of the American government in 1918?

Law-making powers were shared between the federal (central) and state governments in 3 main ways:

- ☑ The federal government in Washington DC was responsible for foreign policy, war, trade between states and the currency.
- ☑ The state governments were responsible for education, marriage laws, trade within the state and local government.
- ☑ The federal and state governments shared control of law and order, the courts, taxes, banks, and public welfare.

How was the American government structured?

Power in the federal government was divided between 3 branches - the executive (president), legislature (Congress) and judiciary (courts).

- ☑ The president (executive) suggested laws, ran foreign policy and the army, and appointed government ministers.
- ☑ Congress (legislature) was split into two houses: the Senate and the House of Representatives. They passed laws, agreed taxes and endorsed the president's appointments of judges and ministers.
- ☑ The Supreme Court (the judiciary) interpreted laws and the constitution and was the highest court of appeal for people to question decisions by the government and courts.

What checks and balances are there in the American government?

The US government was arranged to make sure no single group could take over or have too much power over the others in 4 main ways:

- ☑ The president could veto laws by Congress, but Congress could override the veto with a two-thirds majority. Congress could also withhold taxes or stop the president from appointing judges or ministers.
- ☑ The president could appoint judges for the Supreme Court, but the Supreme Court could stop the president's actions if it decided they were unconstitutional.
- ☑ Congress could override Supreme Court judgements by passing amendments to change the constitution, but the Supreme Court could say Congress's other laws were unconstitutional.

- Congress could remove a president from office due to acts of treason, bribery or another high crime; this is known as impeachment.

How can a president be impeached within the American government?
There are 4 key stages to impeach a president.
- Impeachment proceedings can begin if it is believed the president has committed treason, bribery or another high crime.
- First, Congress investigates the accusations.
- Then, the House of Representatives passes articles of impeachment.
- Finally, Congress puts the accused president on trial. If they vote by a two-thirds majority that the president is guilty, the president is removed from office.

Which political parties were there in the American government in 1918?
By 1918, there were 2 main political parties in America:
- The Republicans, who wanted businesses to succeed.
- The Democrats, who wanted a solution to America's social problems.

Who are the Republicans in American government?
In 1918, the Republicans wanted to see businesses succeed and believed the government should only play a small role in running the country.

Who are the Democrats in American government?
In 1918, the Democrats wanted the government to play a larger role in running America in order to solve the country's social problems.

How do state governments work within the American government?
Like the federal government, state governments were divided into executive, legislature and judicial branches.
- The executive branch was headed by a governor, elected by the people.
- The legislature usually had two houses, a Senate and a House of Representatives, to vote on laws and the state budget.
- The state judicial branch was led by the state Supreme Court.

DID YOU KNOW?

3 interesting facts about the American Constitution:
- ✓ The Constitution contains 4,534 words.
- ✓ Four of the Constitution's signatories were born in Ireland.
- ✓ It is the shortest written Constitution of any major country in the world.

US POLITICAL SYSTEM

'With all its faults, the American political system is the freest and most democratic in the world.' - Eldridge Cleaver

What was the political system in the USA after the Second World War?

Each state has its own government. The federal government, based in Washington DC, governs the whole country.

> **DID YOU KNOW?**
>
> **It's possible for a presidential candidate to win the popular vote but lose the overall election through the electoral college system.**
>
> This happened with both Al Gore in 2000 and Hillary Clinton in 2016.

COLD WAR

The Cold War originated in the ideological conflict between capitalism and communism.

What was the Cold War?

The Cold War was a state of hostility that existed between the USSR and the USA in the second half of the 20th century.

What is the definition of a cold war?

A cold war is a conflict in which there is no direct fighting between the two sides. It is fought through economic and political actions.

When was the Cold War?

The Cold War lasted from 1945 to 1991.

Who was involved in the Cold War?

The Cold War was between the USA and its allies, and the Soviet Union, its satellite states and its allies.

What were the long-term causes of the Cold War?

There are 7 main reasons the Cold War happened:

- ☑ In October 1917, the Bolsheviks seized power in Russia. By 1921 they had created the first communist state. They were anti-capitalism and wanted to spread the communist revolution across the world.
- ☑ America and Britain did not trust the USSR as Russia had withdrawn from the First World War in 1917, despite being a member of the Triple Entente with Britain and France.
- ☑ The USSR did not trust the USA, France and Britain because they sent troops to fight against the Bolsheviks in the Russian Civil War.
- ☑ In the 1920s, the USA suffered from the First Red Scare and was hostile towards the USSR.
- ☑ The USSR was angry it was not recognised as a country by the USA until 1933.
- ☑ The relationship between the USSR and the West deteriorated before the Second World War. The Soviet Union was angry at not being invited to the Munich Conference in 1938.
- ☑ When the USSR signed the Nazi-Soviet Pact in 1939, Britain and France were horrified.

How was the Cold War fought?

The Cold War was fought in 7 key ways:

- Propaganda.
- Spying or espionage, such as using spy planes to take photographs.
- An arms race to have the most developed weapons, particularly nuclear missiles.
- A space race competing for success in space, such as being the first nation to put a man on the moon.
- Financial aid or loans to other countries to gain their support.
- Proxy wars, where the USA and the USSR became involved in conflicts in other countries. An example is the Korean War *(p.26)* of 1950-53.
- Threats made by either side.

What created tension between the Soviet Union and the USA at the beginning of the Cold War?

The ideological differences between the superpowers created tension between them. The Soviet Union supported communism, whereas the USA and Britain were capitalist countries.

What were the different ideologies in the Cold War?

The Cold War was a result of ideological differences between the two sides:

- The USSR was communist. Communism is a system where there is no private ownership of land, property or business. The aim is to achieve economic equality for the benefit of the people through central control of the state economy.
- The USA was capitalist. Capitalism is a system where individuals are free to own land, property and businesses to create wealth and accept there will be economic inequality as a result.

Why were the USA and the USSR considered superpowers during the Cold War?

The USSR and the USA were considered to be superpowers because they possessed 3 key things:

- Massive military might, including nuclear weapons.
- Economic might.
- The ability to dominate other countries.

Why was Stalin distrustful of Truman at the beginning at the Cold War?

Joseph Stalin was distrustful of Harry S Truman for 3 key reasons:

- Truman was anti-communist.
- He tried to control the Potsdam meeting.
- He successfully tested the atomic bomb without consulting Stalin and used it in the Hiroshima and Nagasaki bombings in the days after Potsdam.

DID YOU KNOW?

The capitalist west was terrified when Russia became a communist state after the October Revolution of 1917.

SATELLITE STATES

After the Second World War, Stalin insisted on a protective 'buffer' of satellite states for the USSR.

What were the Soviet satellite states?
The Soviet satellite states were countries in eastern Europe under the political, economic and military influence of the USSR.

Who were the Soviet satellite states?
They were Poland, Czechoslovakia, Hungary, Romania, Bulgaria and East Germany.

When were the Soviet satellite states created?
The satellite states were created between 1946 and 1949.

What methods were used to create the Soviet satellite states?
There are 2 key things to note about the methods used:
- In the late 1940s, Stalin installed communist leaders in eastern European countries using 'salami tactics'.
- The term 'salami tactics' was coined by the communist Hungarian leader, Matyas Rakosi, to describe how Stalin dealt with opposition 'slice by slice'.

How were the Soviet satellite states created?
There were 5 main ways in which the Soviet Union took over eastern European countries:
- The Red Army supported communists and intimidated the opposition. They acted as an occupying force.
- Elections were held and as a result the communists were part of coalition governments.
- The communists worked in coalitions to undermine the government and held key positions, such as head of the police, so they could arrest and murder opponents.
- Propaganda was used to label any opposition party or leader a fascist to boost support for communist parties or to demonise democratic politicians.
- Once in government, communist parties, aided by the security forces, rigged elections to ensure they remained in power.

What was the importance of the Soviet satellite states?
The satellite states helped the Soviet Union in 4 key ways:
- It meant the USSR had gained a large territory with which it could trade.
- They enhanced its power.
- In theory, they strengthened communism.
- They acted as a buffer zone to protect the USSR from invasion.

What were the different points of view about the Soviet satellite states?
There are 2 key things to note about how satellite states are viewed:
- Stalin viewed the satellite states as a necessary buffer against future invasion from Germany in particular.
- However, Britain and the USA saw them as a threat to the West.

> **DID YOU KNOW?**
>
> The countries of eastern Europe were called satellite states in the West because they were effectively controlled by the USSR and were positioned close around its border, like satellites around a planet.

IRON CURTAIN SPEECH, 1946

'From Stettin in the Baltic, to Trieste in the Adriatic, an iron curtain has descended across the continent.' - Winston Churchill 1947

What was the 'Iron Curtain' speech?

Winston Churchill, although no longer the prime minister of Britain, gave a significant speech where he described how Europe had been divided by an 'iron curtain'. This analogy described the USSR's actions in eastern Europe that had divided Europe in two.

When was the 'Iron Curtain' speech delivered?

Winston Churchill gave the speech in March 1946.

Who delivered the 'Iron Curtain' speech?

Winston Churchill gave the 'Iron Curtain' speech.

Where was the 'Iron Curtain' speech delivered?

Winston Churchill gave the speech in Fulton, USA.

What important argument was made by Churchill during the 'Iron Curtain' speech?

Churchill argued that:

- Strong American-British relations were essential to stop the spread of communism and maintain peace.
- The USA must play an active role in world affairs.

Why was the 'Iron Curtain' speech important?

It helped bolster American and western European opposition to communism and the Soviet Union. It worsened relations between the USSR and the West.

How did Stalin respond to the 'Iron Curtain' speech?

Stalin responded to the 'Iron Curtain' speech by:

- Comparing Churchill to Hitler and claiming Churchill was attempting to draw racial boundaries.
- Calling Churchill a warmonger (someone who encourages or seeks war).

> **DID YOU KNOW?**
>
> Some regard Churchill's 'Iron Curtain' speech as the real beginning of the Cold War, because it was one of the first public announcements of hostility.

Get our free app at GCSEHistory.com

TRUMAN DOCTRINE, 1947

'The seeds of totalitarian regimes are nurtured by misery and want. They spread and grow in the evil soil of poverty and strife.' - Harry Truman

What was the Truman Doctrine?

The Truman Doctrine was an American policy which was anti-communist and involved the containment of communism. It led to the Marshall Plan *(p.23)*.

When did the Truman Doctrine begin?

President Harry S Truman announced his doctrine on 12th March, 1947.

Why was the Truman Doctrine established?

There were 3 main reasons the Truman Doctrine was created:

- Britain could not afford to give any more military support to the Greek government in the civil war against Greek communists.
- The USA promised $400 million in aid to Greece and Turkey to help win the war against the Greek communists.
- It aimed to contain the spread of communism by giving military and economic assistance to any country threatened by communism.

What were the main points of the Truman Doctrine?

The Truman Doctrine contained 3 key points:

- It stated the world had a choice between communism, or capitalism and democracy;
- The USA would send troops and economic aid to countries threatened by communism so it was contained and could not spread;
- The USA would no longer follow an isolationist foreign policy and would now get involved in the affairs of other countries, rather than stay out of them.

What conditions were there in order for countries to receive aid under the Truman Doctrine?

Countries had to choose capitalism over communism in order to receive aid from the USA.

What was the importance of the Truman Doctrine?

There were 4 main reasons the Truman Doctrine was important:

- It meant the USA officially abandoned its isolationist foreign policy and would play an active role in the world.
- It meant the USA was on a potential collision course with the USSR as the doctrine was directed against the spread of communism.
- It directly resulted in the creation of the Marshall Plan *(p.23)*.
- It resulted in the further deterioration in the relationship between the USA and the USSR.

DID YOU KNOW?

Harry S Truman's middle name was, literally, 'S'.
It was included to honour his grandfathers, who both had 'S' in their names.

MARSHALL PLAN, 1947

'Our policy is directed not against any country or doctrine but against hunger, poverty, desperation and chaos.' - Harry Truman

What was the Marshall Plan?
The Marshall Plan was a scheme to provide economic aid to Europe.

When was the Marshall Plan introduced?
The Marshall Plan was introduced in 1948.

Who came up with the Marshall Plan?
It was proposed by the US Secretary of State, George C Marshall.

Why was the Marshall Plan introduced?
The Marshall Plan was essentially the Truman Doctrine *(p.22)* in action. By making countries dependent on US dollars, it would prevent the spread of communism.

How much money was provided by the Marshall Plan?
$13.3 billion was provided by the USA to help rebuild Europe.

Which countries received aid under the Marshall Plan?
A total of 16 western European countries, including France, West Germany and Britain, received aid.

What was it hoped would be achieved by the Marshall Plan?
It was feared the damage and poverty caused by the Second World War would encourage people to turn to communism. Giving countries money to rebuild would stop them becoming communist.

What were the conditions needed to receive aid from the Marshall Plan?
In order to receive money, countries had to trade with the USA and be capitalist.

What was the reaction to the Marshall Plan?
The USSR reacted in 4 main ways to the Marshall Plan:
- The Soviet Union saw both the Truman Doctrine *(p.22)* and the Marshall Plan as a threat to communism.
- Stalin called it 'dollar imperialism' and claimed the USA was trying to take over Europe using its economic strength.
- Stalin responded by creating Cominform in 1947, which coordinated and controlled communist parties in Europe from the USSR.
- Comecon was established in 1949 to organise economic trade between eastern Europe and the USSR.

What was the significance of the Marshall Plan?
The Marshall Plan was significant for 4 key reasons:
- It helped the economic recovery of western Europe.
- It limited the expansion of Soviet influence in Europe so the USSR was 'contained'.
- It deepened the divide between western Europe and eastern Europe as they were now divided politically and economically.
- It worsened the relationship between the USA and the USSR.

> **DID YOU KNOW?**
>
> If the USA spent the same proportion of its GDP on aid today as it did during the Marshall Plan, the expenditure would amount to $800 billion dollars.

BERLIN BLOCKADE, 1948-49

The Berlin Blockade by Stalin was designed to establish dominance over Berlin and Germany.

What was the Berlin Blockade?

The USSR closed all road, rail and river transport links into West Berlin. This stopped all supplies getting into the city. British, French and US troops were asked to leave.

When was the Berlin Blockade?

The Berlin Blockade started in June 1948 and ended in May 1949.

What caused the Berlin Blockade?

There were 8 key causes of the Berlin Blockade:

- The growing tension between the USA and the USSR over the future of Germany.
- The growing tension between the USA and the USSR because of their ideological differences and the start of the Cold War *(p.18)*.
- In January 1947, the British and USA joined their zones, creating 'Bizonia'. This broke the agreements made at the Potsdam Conference.
- In December 1947, at the London Conference, Britain, France and the USA met to discuss Germany and decide Germany's new constitution. The USSR was not included.
- In March 1948, France's zone joined Bizonia to create 'Trizonia'.
- The USSR left the Allied Control Commission, accusing the West of breaking the Potsdam agreements. They were angry the London Conference had taken place.
- In April 1948, Trizonia started to receive Marshall Aid *(p.23)* and began to rebuild.
- Britain, France and the USA introduced a new 'safe' currency, the Deutschmark, into Trizonia on 23rd June, 1948, which angered the USSR.

What were the consequences of the Berlin Blockade?

There were 3 main consequences of the Berlin Blockade:

- It prevented supplies reaching West Berlin.
- It led to the Berlin Airlift *(p.25)* from June 1948 to May 1949, in which the Western powers used airplanes to fly supplies into West Berlin.
- The relationship between the USSR and the West deteriorated further, eventually leading to the creation of NATO.

What was the significance of the Berlin Blockade?

The Berlin Blockade was significant for 2 key reasons:

- The West saw it as an act of aggression by Stalin.
- It created the first major crisis between the USA and the USSR in the Cold War *(p.18)*.

Quizzes, amazing exam preparation tools and more at GCSEHistory.com

> **DID YOU KNOW?**
>
> The blockade lasted 318 days (11 months).

BERLIN AIRLIFT, 1948-49

Rather than risk war over the Blockade, the Americans circumnavigated it with the Berlin Airlift.

What did the western powers do in response to the Berlin Blockade?

Western powers responded to the blockade of West Berlin by organising an airlift. Supplies were flown into West Berlin every day.

When was the Berlin Airlift?

The Berlin Airlift saw supplies flown into Berlin every day from 26th June, 1948, to 12th May, 1949.

Why did the Berlin Airlift happen?

There were 3 main reasons the Berlin Airlift occurred:

- The West did not want to be forced out of West Berlin because Stalin would be able to take over.
- The USA wanted to contain communism, as promised in the Truman Doctrine *(p.22)*.
- It was a way to get around the blockade without starting a war.

What happened during the Berlin Airlift?

There were 3 key events during the Berlin Airlift:

- Britain, France and the USA flew in supplies of food, medicine and fuel throughout the Blockade.
- By the end of the Blockade, approximately 8,000 tonnes of supplies were being flown in every day.
- A new airport called Berlin-Tegel was built and a new runway was built at Berlin-Tempelhof to cope with the number of planes flying in supplies.

What were the consequences of the Berlin Airlift?

There were 4 key consequences of the Berlin Airlift:

- Two Germanies were created; The Federal Republic of Germany (West Germany) in May 1949 and the German Democratic Republic (East Germany) in October 1949.
- It led to the USA creating a military alliance called NATO in April 1949.
- Europe was divided even more: politically (capitalism versus communism), economically (Marshall Aid *(p.23)* versus Comecon), and now militarily.
- The balance of power became more unstable when the USSR conducted its first successful atomic bomb test in August 1949.

> **DID YOU KNOW?**
>
> The Americans airlifted a total of 2,245,315 tons of supplies into Berlin during the airlift.

SOVIET UNION NUCLEAR WEAPONS

'I think the bomb instead constitutes merely a first step in a new control by man over the forces of nature too revolutionary and dangerous to fit into old concepts'. - Henry Stimson

What was the arms race?
The arms race was a competition between the USA and the USSR to gain military dominance by developing their nuclear capabilities and weapons.

When was the arms race?
The Soviet Union emerged as a nuclear power in 1949, leading to the arms race with the USA. This lasted until the end of the Cold War *(p.18)* in 1990.

What was the importance of the arms race?
The arms race was important for 2 main reasons:
- It led to the fear of mutually assured destruction as both sides had enough weapons to destroy the world many times over.
- The USA and the USSR had to find ways to solve disputes that did not result in a nuclear war.

What were the most important events of the arms race?
There were 6 main military achievements and events during the arms race:
- 1945 - the USA dropped atomic bombs on Hiroshima and Nagasaki, bringing the Second World War to an end.
- 1949 - the USSR tested an atomic bomb.
- 1952 - the USA developed the hydrogen bomb.
- 1953 - the USSR tested its own hydrogen bomb.
- 1957 - both the USA and USSR successfully tested intercontinental ballistic missiles (ICBMs).
- 1962 - the Cuban Missile Crisis was the highest point of tension in the arms race.

KOREAN WAR, 1950-53

America was very concerned when the Korean War began, as it appeared to confirm the spread of communism.

What was the Korean War?
The Korean War was fought between North and South Korea and was the first flashpoint of the Cold War in Asia.

Where did the Korean War take place?
In Korea, which is between China to the west and Japan to the east.

When was the Korean War?
The Korean War began in June 1950 and finished in 1954.

What were the key phases of the Korean War?
There were 5 main phases to the war, including:

- North Korea invaded South Korea on 25th June, 1950.
- A UN army, made up mostly of American military and led by General Douglas MacArthur, arrived in Korea in September 1950 to push back against the North Korean invasion.
- In October 1950, UN forces advanced into North Korean territory.
- On 25th October, China entered the war. Together with the North Korean army, they pushed the UN forces back below the 38th parallel. This resulted in a stalemate for over two years.
- After peace talks on 27th July, 1953, the UN, China and North Korea signed a peace treaty.

What were the long-term causes that led to the Korean War?

Several important long-term events led to the Korean War, including:

- The history of Korea was shaped by many wars over who would control it. Both China and Japan ruled the nation for significant periods of time.
- Between 1910 and 1945, Korea was controlled by Japan. This changed at the end of the Second World War.
- At the end of the Second World War, the Japanese in the north surrendered to the USSR, and those in the south to the USA.

At the end of the Second World War, what was the situation that led to the Korean War?

At the end of the Second World War, when Japan surrendered and Korea was occupied by Soviet troops in the north and American troops in the south, the following happened:

- The country was divided into two separate zones along the 38th parallel, a circle of latitude that runs across the middle of Korea.
- The division of Korea was supposed to be temporary. The aim was for it to be a united and independent country. The United Nations was to organise elections that would achieve this.
- Instead of free elections, the Soviets in North Korea enabled Korean communist Kim Il-Sung to take control of the nation without being elected.
- There was an election in US-controlled South Korea, and USA supporter and capitalist figure Syngman Rhee became its leader.
- At this point, North and South Korea became two different nations. The USSR zone in the north became the People's Republic of Korea, and the US zone in the south became the Republic of Korea.
- While the leaders in both North and South Korea were nationalists and wanted a united country after the war, they wanted the nation to be led by different ideologies - capitalism in the south and communism in the north.

Who ran North Korea at the time of the Korean War?

After 1947, the government in North Korea was the communist Democratic People's Republic led by Kim Il-Sung. The capital was Pyongyang.

Who ran South Korea at the time of the Korean War?

After 1947, the government in South Korea was the non-communist Republic of Korea led by Syngman Rhee. Its capital was Seoul.

What were the key events in the build-up to the Korean War?

The leaders of North and South Korea each saw themselves as the legitimate and rightful ruler of the whole nation. Events in the build-up to the Korean War included:

- Due to the attitude of superiority from both sides there were a number of clashes on the border between North and South Korea.
- Kim Il-Sung, the leader of North Korea, visited Stalin in 1949 to ask for his support in an invasion of South Korea. He felt this would be welcome in the south as an effort to reunite the two nations.
- Stalin did not think it was the right time as he did not want a fight against US troops still stationed in South Korea.

- In 1950, Stalin's circumstances had changed. The US troops had left South Korea; communists were in power in China; and the USSR had its own nuclear weapons and had cracked the secret codes used by the USA to talk to other nations. As a result, Stalin felt any future actions in Korea would not meet American opposition.
- Stalin began sending tanks, artillery and aircraft to North Korea and gave the go-ahead for an invasion of the south.
- Stalin stated USSR soldiers would not be directly involved, and if further supplies were needed North Korea should ask China.

What started the Korean War?

The Korean War broke out when North Korea invaded South Korea on 25th June, 1950.

Why did the UN get involved in the Korean War?

When the south was invaded, the USA brought the matter to the UN which passed a resolution calling for North Korea to withdraw. When it did not, the UN sent international troops - mostly American - to force it out. In this way the USA could argue it was acting against international aggression rather than following its containment policy.

Why did America get involved in the Korean War?

There were 3 key reasons America got involved in the Korean War:

- President Truman was concerned communism was spreading in Asia.
- China's fall to communism in 1949 heightened this fear.
- Truman was also concerned about Stalin's use of Cominform to encourage countries to turn to communism.

What was America's role in the Korean War?

America had 2 main roles in the Korean War:

- United Nations troops, mainly American and led by US General Douglas MacArthur, were sent to Korea. The North was supported by the Soviet Union.
- UN forces were able to push North Korea back to the Chinese border, but in late 1950 China joined the war and the UN had to retreat.

What ended the Korean War?

After three years of fighting an armistice was agreed, which re-established the border between North and South Korea.

What effect did the Korean War have on America?

There were 5 main consequences of the Korean War:

- It demonstrated the USA's commitment to containing communism and led to a tripling of military spending to prevent its spread.
- To stop the spread of communism in Asia, the Southeast Asia Treaty Organisation (SEATO) was set up in September 1954. Britain, Pakistan, USA, Thailand, France, Australia, the Philippines and New Zealand all joined.
- The sacking of General MacArthur over his proposal to deploy nuclear bombs against North Korea underlined the USA's caution with regard to using nuclear weapons.
- The Soviet Union doubled the size of the Red Army, from 2.8 million in 1950 to 5.6 million in 1955.
- As the war did not escalate further, it showed neither superpower was prepared to engage in direct military confrontation with the other, preferring instead to fight proxy wars.

DID YOU KNOW?

3 facts about the Korean War:
- ✔ The Korean War involved many different nations including the USSR, China, America and 21 countries fighting as part of a UN force.
- ✔ Korea is still divided today; the North is a communist dictatorship.
- ✔ Korea is still technically at war as a peace treaty has never been signed.

RED SCARE

'Now I am going to tell you how we are not going to fight communism. We are not going to transform our fine FBI into a Gestapo secret police. That is what some people would like to do.' - Harry Truman

What was the Red Scare?

The Red Scare was a time when many Americans were afraid of new political ideas and therefore suspicious of new immigrants. There have been two Red Scares in America. The first took place between 1919 - 1920. The second began at the end of the Second World War and lasted until the mid-1950s.

THE 1950S RED SCARE

'No one man can terrorize a whole nation unless we are all his accomplices.' - Ed Murrow on Senator McCarthy

What was the Second Red Scare?

After the Second World War, many people in America believed the communists were trying to take over America. It led to the Second Red Scare, with thousands of people put on trial and losing their jobs, often with very little proof.

When did the Second Red Scare happen?

The Second Red Scare was in the 1940s and 1950s.

What did the FBI do during the Second Red Scare?

The FBI, or Federal Bureau of Investigation, was anti-communist and played a big part in arresting those suspected of communism during the First Red Scare of 1919-20. As the Cold War *(p.18)* began, they once again began collecting information on those they suspected of spying for the Soviet Union.

What did the Federal Loyalty Boards do during the Second Red Scare?

The Federal Loyalty Boards were created to investigate government employees to see if they were communists or had links to communism.

How many people did the Federal Loyalty Boards investigate during the second Red Scare?

3 million government employees were investigated between 1947 and 1951; approximately 3,000 were sacked or made to resign from their jobs.

What was the role of HUAC during the Second Red Scare?

HUAC, or the House Committee on Un-American Activities, had 2 main roles:

- It was created in 1938 to monitor any groups suspected of activities believed to be 'un-American'.
- From 1947, it began public hearings on the threat posed by the Communist Party of America. Suspected communists and witnesses were questioned and, depending on their responses, sent for trial.

What happened to the Hollywood Ten during the Second Red Scare?

The Hollywood Ten *(p.31)*:

- Consisted of 10 Hollywood writers, producers and directors questioned by HUAC about communism within the film industry.
- Refused to answer any questions using the First Amendment of the US Constitution.
- Were jailed for one year and blacklisted from working in Hollywood.

What was the role of Alger Hiss during the Second Red Scare?

Alger Hiss *(p.32)* was important during the Second Red Scare for 3 main reasons:

- He was a member of the state department who was accused of passing information to the Soviet Union.
- In 1949, he was put on trial and sentenced to 5 years in prison for lying to the court. Although he was never convicted of spying, many thought he must have been guilty of something.
- During the Hiss trial, the Soviet Union tested its first atomic bomb, heightening fears over communism.

What did the Rosenbergs do during the Second Red Scare?

The 4 key details of the Rosenberg *(p.33)* case were:

- A married couple were accused of spying for the Soviet Union and passing secrets about the atomic bomb.
- They were found guilty in March 1951 and executed in June 1953.
- Some Americans thought the Rosenbergs were innocent, but many more believed they were responsible for helping the Soviet Union make its first atomic bomb.
- The case caused great fear in America, particularly as the couple's arrest coincided with the outbreak of the Korean War *(p.26)*.

What did the McCarran Act do during the Second Red Scare?

The Second Red Scare had 2 main results:

- The McCarran Act was passed in August 1950, requiring all communist organisations to register with the government.
- The Act was strengthened in 1952, banning communists from holding US passports or having certain jobs.

What was McCarthy's role in the Second Red Scare?

Joseph McCarthy *(p.34)* was a Republican senator. He conducted a powerful campaign against alleged communists which became known as the McCarthy witch hunts. He was widely believed at first, as Americans were worried about 'Reds under the bed', but his claims were later proven false.

DID YOU KNOW?

Much of the Red Scare had public support.

By the end of 1949, 68% of Americans believed the Communist Party should be banned.

HOLLYWOOD TEN, 1947

'The Constitution was never intended to cloak or shield those who would destroy it.' - J Parnell Thomas, Chairman of HUAC

Who were the Hollywood Ten?

The Hollywood Ten were a group of producers and writers who were investigated because they were believed to be communists. The group included Alvah Bessie, John Howard Lawson and Dalton Trumbo.

When were the Hollywood Ten under investigation?

The Hollywood Ten case was in 1947.

What were the Hollywood Ten accused of?

The Hollywood Ten were accused of being communist and using their positions in Hollywood to spread communist views.

What happened at the trial of the Hollywood Ten?

There were 4 main events during the Hollywood Ten case:

- The House of Un-American Activities Committee was investigating suspected communist influence in Hollywood and called the Hollywood Ten to answer questions.
- All 10 directors and writers refused to answer any questions, in line with their rights under the First Amendment.
- They were found in contempt of Congress in April 1948.
- They were each fined $1,000 and sent to prison for 1 year.

What were the consequences of the Hollywood Ten case?

There were 3 main consequences of the Hollywood Ten case:

- Loyalty boards were set up by the FBI to investigate government workers, as the case created fear there were more 'Reds' working in powerful positions.
- The Hollywood Ten served their time in prison and were blacklisted so they could not work in Hollywood. However, some did continue to work under 'pen names', or assumed names.
- The number of people in Hollywood investigated for being communist grew and so did the blacklist. All those listed were unable to work in the entertainment industry any longer, so their careers were ruined.

DID YOU KNOW?

Some of the Hollywood Ten continued to work, but under aliases.

Lester Cole wrote the screenplay to the film Born Free under the name of Gerald L C Copley.

ALGER HISS CASE, 1948 TO 1950

'I am confident that in the future the full facts of how Whittaker Chambers was able to carry out forgery by typewriter will be disclosed.' - Alger Hiss at his trial

Who was Alger Hiss?
Alger Hiss was an ex-adviser to President Roosevelt who was accused of being a communist during the Second Red Scare *(p.29)*.

When was Alger Hiss put on trial?
Alger Hiss was accused in 1948. His first trial was in August 1949 and his second trial was in January 1950.

What was Alger Hiss accused of?
Alger Hiss was accused of being a member of the Communist Party and spying on America for the USSR.

What happened during the trial of Alger Hiss?
There were 3 main events during his trials:
- Whittaker Chambers, an ex-member of the Communist Party, claimed in a HUAC hearing that Alger Hiss was a communist who was spying when he worked for President Roosevelt and passed on government documents.
- Hiss appeared before HUAC and was put on trial.
- At the second trial in 1950, Hiss was found guilty of perjury - lying to the court. He was charged for lying about giving government documents to Chambers.

What punishment did Alger Hiss receive?
Alger Hiss was sentenced to 5 years in prison for perjury.

What happened during the trial of Alger Hiss that affected the case?
During his case the USSR tested its first atomic bomb. This resulted in a heightened fear the Soviets had gained nuclear secrets by spying in America, and that Soviet spies occupied powerful positions in the USA.

What were the results of the Alger Hiss case?
There were 2 main consequences of the Alger Hiss case:
- The Second Red Scare *(p.29)* continued to grow.
- The government passed the McCarran Act in 1950. This meant Communist Party members could not hold an American passport or work in the defence industries. Any communist organisations also had to be registered with the government.

DID YOU KNOW?

Alger Hiss maintained his innocence until the day he died.

ROSENBERG CASE, 1951

'I consider your crime worse than murder.' - Judge Kaufman at the Rosenbergs' trial

Who were the Rosenbergs?

Ethel and Julius Rosenberg were a married couple. Julius was an engineer working for the US Army Signal Corps. They were put on trial during the Second Red Scare *(p.29)*.

When were the Rosenbergs put on trial?

The trial of the Rosenbergs started on 6th March, 1951.

What were the Rosenbergs accused of?

The Rosenbergs were accused of spying for the USSR and passing on nuclear secrets.

What was the evidence against the Rosenbergs?

There were 3 main things to note about the evidence against the Rosenbergs:

- It came from decoding Soviet telegrams in which the Rosenbergs were not directly named, but code names were used.
- It was Ethel's own brother, David Greenglass, who named Julius and Ethel as spies. Initially he only named Julius but later claimed his sister was involved, supposedly to save his own wife.
- There is much debate about exactly what happened. It is likely Julius was spying and Ethel was innocent.

What events affected the trial of the Rosenbergs?

During the Rosenberg trial, the Korean War *(p.26)* had started, increasing Cold War *(p.18)* tension. The Second Red Scare *(p.29)* was escalating.

How were the Rosenbergs punished?

On 5th April, 1951, Ethel and Julius Rosenberg were sentenced to death. They were electrocuted on 19th June, 1953.

What happened after the Rosenbergs sentence?

There were 2 main consequences of the Rosenberg case:

- There were protests in support of the Rosenbergs because they had received the death sentence. To some people, it seemed an excessive punishment.
- The Second Red Scare *(p.29)* intensified and created the climate in which Senator McCarthy could accuse many people of being communists.

DID YOU KNOW?

The spy who passed nuclear secrets to the USSR only received 14 years in prison - a far more lenient punishment than the Rosenbergs received.

MCCARTHYISM

'This is the first time in my experience that I ever heard of a senator trying to discredit his own government before the world.' - President Harry Truman, 1950

Who was Senator McCarthy?
Joseph McCarthy was a Republican senator from Wisconsin. From 1950 to 1954, he conducted a powerful campaign against alleged communists.

When was McCarthy active?
Joseph McCarthy was active between 1950 and 1954.

Why did people believe McCarthy?
McCarthy was helped by events outside America. China, for example, turned communist in 1949 and many people were fearful of a communist takeover. As a result McCarthy won a lot of support, with thousands attending his speeches and millions watching his television appearances.

How did McCarthy investigate people?
McCarthy used 2 main methods:
- McCarthy held public hearings where he used bullying and aggressive questioning to try and get people to confess.
- He attacked high-profile figures and anybody who spoke out against him was accused of being either a communist or a communist sympathiser.

What were the main events McCarthy was involved in?
Senator McCarthy was involved in 5 key events:
- In February 1950, he claimed to have a list containing the names of 205 Communist Party members who worked in the US government *(p. 16)*.
- Following this, the Tydings Committee investigated his claims.
- In 1954, his hearings on communist influence in the American army were televised.
- In March 1954, McCarthy was criticised on the Ed Murrow show because of hearings attacking the US Army.
- In December 1954, he was censured by the Senate for 'improper conduct'.

How many people did McCarthy accuse?
McCarthy claimed he had a list of 205 Communist Party members who worked in the US State Department. He later changed the figure to 57.

How were McCarthy's claims investigated?
There were 3 main events relating to the Tydings Committee:
- In February 1950, McCarthy's claims were investigated by the Tydings Committee led by Senator Tydings. The committee discovered his accusations to be false.
- Senator Tydings was accused of being 'un-American' and a communist sympathiser by McCarthy. McCarthy even created fake evidence against Tydings to discredit him.
- Tydings was not re-elected later that year.

How did McCarthy attack the US Army?
There were 3 key events that happened when McCarthy attacked the US Army:
- In autumn 1953, McCarthy led a new Senate sub-committee on communist influence in the US Army.

- When the televised hearings began, many were horrified at his bullying.
- The army also responded to his accusations by providing evidence which showed McCarthy had abused his position.

Why did people stop believing McCarthy?

There were 4 main reasons for McCarthy's downfall:
- In the autumn of 1953, McCarthy led an attack on the US Army which led to people criticising his actions.
- Vice-President Nixon criticised McCarthy's methods in a radio broadcast.
- In March 1954, broadcast journalist Ed Murrow did an episode of his popular weekly news show about McCarthy. Ed Murrow criticised him by using TV footage of his speeches and methods.
- In December 1954, McCarthy was censured by the Senate for 'improper conduct'.

When did McCarthy lose support?

In the mid-1950s, McCarthy's importance began to decline and he was widely criticised. He lost his power after he was censured by the Senate in December 1954.

What effect did McCarthy have on America?

America was affected in 2 main ways by McCarthy's actions:
- The lives of thousands of people who lost their jobs or had their careers destroyed by his allegations were ruined.
- McCarthyism affected nearly every American. Thousands reported people they suspected of being communists. Those who held different opinions or political ideas were accused of being communists by others, and fewer people joined trade unions.

DID YOU KNOW?

McCarthy had support from businessmen and newspapers.

Newsmen at the Chicago Tribune sometimes wrote his speeches and several wealthy Texans donated large amounts in support.

TREATMENT OF BLACK AMERICANS

'Our constitution is colour-blind, and neither knows nor tolerates classes among citizens.' - Judge Harlan, disagreeing with Plessy v Ferguson

What was the experience of African Americans in the USA in the 1950s?

Life for African Americans in 1950s America depended on where they lived. Most southern states had some segregations laws, which meant black and white people had to use separate facilities.

What was life like for African Americans in the south in the 1950s?

In the south, strict segregation laws known as the 'Jim Crow' laws were enforced. This meant African Americans had to attend different schools to white children, use separate facilities in public areas, and were separated from white people on public transport.

What were the Jim Crow laws for for African Americans during the 1950s?

The 'Jim Crow' laws were introduced in a number of southern states to keep African Americans apart from white people. They were still in force after the Second World War.

What was life like for African Americans living in the north in the 1950s?

African Americans in the north of America faced 4 main issues:

- Racism and discrimination were common.
- Most African Americans lived in areas where there were no white people, they self-segregated, and they earned less.
- There was a higher rate of unemployment among African Americans.
- African Americans usually lived in the poorest areas.

Why didn't African Americans vote in the 1950s and 1960s?

In the 1950s, few African Americans living in the south were able to vote as state governments used 3 key methods to prevent them from registering:

- Violence was often threatened or used.
- They had to pay a poll tax, which few African Americans could afford.
- They had to pass a literacy test which was deliberately made very difficult. White Americans did not have to take the literacy test.

Why didn't the president help African Americans in the 1950s?

Congress and the president did not enforce civil rights because they sometimes needed support from southern politicians who were often racist. Many southern voters would also not support civil rights.

Why didn't the Supreme Court help African Americans in the 1950s?

There were 2 main reasons the Supreme Court did not ban segregation:

- The Supreme Court could have banned segregation but was heavily influenced by the views and opinions of its judges, many of whom were against civil rights.
- The Supreme Court had ruled in 1896 that separate facilities were allowed as long as they were equal. This was known as the Plessy v Ferguson case. It was used as a legal precedent when any civil rights groups tried to challenge segregation legally.

DID YOU KNOW?

The Plessy v Ferguson case originated from an incident when an African American passenger, Homer Plessy, refused to sit in the carriage for African Americans. The case went all the way to the Supreme Court.

SEGREGATION

'Coloured go to back of bus' - sign in Montgomery, Alabama

How were African Americans segregated in the 1950s?

There was widespread discrimination against, and segregation of, African Americans across the USA in the early 1950s. Access to some facilities, housing, education and life opportunities were either refused or restricted. Segregation was enforced and as a people they were marginalised.

How was segregation enforced in the north of the USA in the 1950s?

In the north they found they were segregated through discrimination in education, employment opportunities and housing. They were only able to get badly paid jobs so could not afford to live anywhere else but the ghettos.

How was segregation enforced in 1950s southern America?

There were 2 main ways segregation was enforced in the south of America.

- A series of state and local laws, known as the 'Jim Crow' laws, were used to legalise and enforce racial segregation.
- African Americans had to attend separate schools and separate areas in places such as restaurants, cinemas, libraries and parks.

Why was segregation an embarrassment to the USA during the Cold war in the 1950s?

During the Cold War (p.18), the USA proclaimed itself as the leading nation of the free world. However, in reality, its black citizens were being treated dreadfully.

Did African Americans have voting rights in America during the period of segregation in the 1950s?

During the 1950s very few African Americans were able to vote in the south.

- In a bid to gain their votes, politicians in the north of the USA began to introduce policies that would appeal to African Americans.
- African Americans in parts of southern states had some voting rights to elect officials within their segregated communities.

What did white people do to prevent African Americans from voting during segregation in the 1950s?

White people employed 5 key methods to try and prevent African Americans from voting:

- African Americans employees were threatened with the loss of their jobs if they tried to vote.
- Some states allowed political parties to block people from being members on the grounds of race.
- In some states, African Americans had to successfully complete complicated literacy tests to be allowed to vote.
- Gangs would congregate outside polling stations to beat up African American voters.
- A number of African American people went to court in an attempt to defend their right to vote. Some of them were murdered.

DID YOU KNOW?

Segregation did not always exist in America.
The key Jim Crow laws emerged between 1890 and 1910.

DISCRIMINATION

'I see what's possible when we recognise that we are one American family, all deserving of equal treatment.' - President Barack Obama

How were African Americans discriminated against in the 1950s?

African Americans suffered discrimination throughout America, but it was worse in some areas of the country.

Where in the Deep South of the USA did discrimination occur?

African Americans were discriminated against in several ways by white people in the Deep South, which was made up of the states in the southern and eastern parts of the USA such as Alabama, Louisiana and Mississippi.

What was discrimination like in the Deep South of the USA?

There are 3 main things to note about how discrimination happened in the Deep South:

- White people refused to socialise with African Americans, seeing them as lazy, stupid and criminally minded.
- There were some racists in law enforcement, including policemen and judges. It was common for African Americans to be beaten unless they confessed to crimes they hadn't carried out, and they could be imprisoned for no reason.
- If an African American was murdered, then often it would not be investigated as the police were often racist and could also be members of the KKK *(p.53)*.

DID YOU KNOW?

In some cases, black adults were even denied the courtesy titles of Mr, Mrs or Miss.

PRESIDENT TRUMAN AND CIVIL RIGHTS

'I believe in the brotherhood of man; not merely the brotherhood of white men, but the brotherhood of all men before the law.' - President Truman

Who was President Truman?

Harry S Truman was the 33rd President of the United States, holding office from 1945 to 1953.

What was an overview of Truman's time as president?

Truman's time as president included the following events:

- He took over from Franklin D Roosevelt during the Second World War.
- He oversaw huge challenges both domestically and internationally as America transitioned from fighting the Second World War in 1945 to the onset of the Cold War *(p.18)* between 1947 and 1949.
- His policy of the Truman Doctrine *(p.22)* and the policy of the containment became the cornerstone of American foreign policy for decades.
- In the years after his presidency he faced huge criticism as the president who 'lost China to communism'.
- He is now considered by historians to be one of America's greatest presidents.

What actions did Truman take in support of civil rights?

President Truman took 2 main actions in support of civil rights:

- In 1946, he set up the 'President's Committee on Civil Rights', which aimed to abolish segregation.
- He ended segregation in the armed forces by issuing executive order 9981 on 26th July, 1948.

What was the impact of President Truman's civil rights policies?

There were 3 main results of President Truman's civil rights policies:

- White people in the southern states were horrified.

- In 1948, some members broke away from the Democrat Party to create the States' Rights Democratic Party, nicknamed the 'Dixiecrats *(p.54)*'.
- It gained President Truman support from African Americans, which helped in the 1948 elections.

> **DID YOU KNOW?**
> Although President Truman pushed for desegregation, he was very critical of the sit-ins that were held in the 1960s.

CIVIL RIGHTS

'There are those who say to you - we are rushing the issue of civil rights. I say we are 172 years late.'
- Hubert Humphrey, 1948

What civil rights organisations were there in the 1950s?

In the 1950s, there were few civil rights organisations. Universities in the north and churches in the south were also involved.

What were the main civil rights organisations in the 1950s?

There were 4 main organisations supporting civil rights in the 1950s.
- The Congress of Racial Equality *(p.40)* (CORE),
- The National Association for the Advancement of Colored People *(p.39)* (NAACP),
- The Regional Council of Negro Leadership *(p.41)* (RCNL).
- The Southern Christian Leadership Conference (SCLC *(p.41)*).

NATIONAL ASSOCIATION FOR THE ADVANCEMENT OF COLORED PEOPLE

'America is race. From its symbolism to its substance, from its founding by slaveholders to its rending by the Civil War.. from Emmett Till to Trayvon Martin.' - former NAACP chairman Julian Bond

What was the NAACP?

The National Association for the Advancement of Colored People was committed to fighting for civil rights in the courts in order to bring an end to segregation.

When was the NAACP set up?

The NAACP was set up in February 1909.

Why was the NAACP created?

The NAACP was set up for 2 main reasons:
- To end the discrimination and violence faced by African Americans.
- To end lynchings of African Americans.

Get our free app at GCSEHistory.com

What events was the NAACP involved in?
The NAACP was involved in 5 key events between the 1940s and 1970s:
- It was involved in challenging segregation in education in the Brown versus Topeka case in 1954.
- It helped protect the witnesses in the Emmett Till *(p.44)* case in 1955.
- It was one of the organisers of the March on Washington *(p.61)* in 1963.
- It was involved in Freedom Summer *(p.62)* of 1964.
- It campaigned for the Civil Rights Act of 1964 and the Voting Rights Act *(p.67)* of 1965.

DID YOU KNOW?

The NAACP is still active today.
It has 2,000 branches across America and is the largest grassroots civil rights organisation.

CONGRESS OF RACIAL EQUALITY

'If i kicked the bucket tomorrow, I would like it to be known that I founded the Congress of Racial Equality in 1942.' - James Farmer

What was CORE?
The Congress of Racial Equality was a non-violent organisation from the north. It used peaceful methods to spread its message and trained others to do so, for example by using boycotts and sit-ins to protest against segregation.

When was CORE set up?
CORE was set up in 1942.

Who were CORE members?
Their membership consisted of African Americans and a significant number of white people.

What events was CORE involved in?
CORE was involved in 5 key events during the civil rights movement:
- In 1955, it helped in the Montgomery Bus Boycott *(p.46)*.
- In 1960, it helped to organise sit-ins.
- In 1961, it organised the Freedom Rides.
- It helped organise the March on Washington *(p.61)* in 1963.
- It organised the Freedom Summer *(p.62)* of 1964.

DID YOU KNOW?

The ideology and tactics of CORE were influenced by Mahatma Gandhi, the Indian independence leader.

REGIONAL COUNCIL OF NEGRO LEADERSHIP

'Guide our people in their civil responsibilities.' - T R M Howard, founder of the RCNL

What was the RCNL?

The Regional Council of Negro Leadership stood against police brutality, campaigned for black rights within segregation and encouraged voter registration. It was active in the state of Mississippi and held several annual civil rights rallies in the 1950s.

When was the RCNL set up?

The Regional Council of Negro Leadership was set up in 1951.

What events was the RCNL involved in?

The Regional Council of Negro Leadership was involved in 3 main events:
- Boycotts of petrol stations (called gas stations in America).
- Voter registration programmes.
- It supported Emmett Till's *(p.44)* family in the trial of his murderers by helping to find evidence to use in court.

> **DID YOU KNOW?**
>
> The first civil rights protest organised by the RCNL was a boycott of petrol (gas) stations.
> The gas stations would not allow black Americans to use their toilets.

SOUTHERN CHRISTIAN LEADERSHIP COUNCIL

'Our lives begin to end the day we become silent about things that matter.' - Martin Luther King

What was the Southern Christian Leadership Council?

The Southern Christian Leadership Council was a civil rights organisation that wanted to redeem the 'soul of America' through non-violent resistance. It was set up to coordinate church-based protest.

When was the SCLC set up?

The SCLC was set up in January 1957.

Who were the leaders of the SCLC?

The SCLC was led by its first president, Martin Luther King, and Ralph Abernathy, a Baptist minister.

What were the main efforts of the SCLC?

The SCLC carried out 2 key activities to further its campaign for equal civil rights.
- The SCLC used non-violent mass action to protest against segregation.
- They gave African Americans training to enable them to pass the voter registration tests.

What events was the SCLC involved in?

There were 4 main events the SCLC was involved in:

- ✓ It organised a voter registration and education project called the Crusade for Citizenship in 1957.
- ✓ It helped to organise the March on Washington *(p.61)* in 1963.
- ✓ The Selma March *(p.66)* to Montgomery in 1965.
- ✓ It organised the Poor People's Campaign *(p.79)* in 1967.

> **DID YOU KNOW?**
>
> The SCLC led a successful campaign for the state of Georgia to change its flag, which contained a Confederate cross - a symbol associated with slavery.

UNIVERSITIES

'I think my experience at the University of Chicago, working in the civil rights movement, did a lot to influence the politics that I have.' - Senator Bernie Sanders

How did universities support the civil rights movement?

Civil rights campaigners were allowed to meet and organise protests at the universities. They also were the site of protests and rallies because students and academics were more likely to be listened to.

CHURCHES

'The philosophy of Christianity is strongly opposed to the underlying philosophy of segregation.' - Martin Luther King, 1957

How did churches support the civil rights movement in the 1950s?

Churches were at the heart of southern communities and were often the central points for marches and protests. They used their funds to finance things like boycotts. They were similar to CORE *(p.40)* in that they tended to use non-violent methods.

How did church leaders support the civil rights movement?

The leaders of the civil rights movement were often also leaders within the black church. They were well-educated people, respected in their communities. They would organise peaceful protests and public speeches.

> **DID YOU KNOW?**
>
> It was the power of the churches in Montgomery that helped legitimise and support the bus boycott.

BROWN V TOPEKA, 1954

'Separate educational facilities are inherently unequal.' - Supreme Court, 1954

What was the Brown v Board of Education case?

Brown v the Board of Education of Topeka was a legal case taken with 4 others to the Supreme Court by the NAACP *(p.39)* to end segregation on the basis it was unconstitutional.

When did the Supreme Court rule on the Brown v Board of Education case?

The Supreme Court gave its verdict on 17th May, 1954.

What were the causes of the Brown v Board of Education case?

There were 3 main reasons the Brown v the Board of Education of Topeka happened:

- In 1951, Linda Brown was not allowed to go to the local all-white summer school because she was black.
- Her father, Oliver Brown, with the support of the NAACP *(p.39)*, brought a case called Brown v Topeka to the local courts in June 1951.
- The court case failed, but the NAACP *(p.39)* and Oliver Brown tried again with 4 other cases.

What happened in the Brown v Board of Education case?

There were 2 main events during Brown v the Board of Education of Topeka:

- Thurgood Marshall, the key NAACP *(p.39)* lawyer, argued that 'separate but equal' was damaging to black American students.
- The judges, led by Chief Justice Warren, were convinced by his arguments and ruled unanimously that segregation was unconstitutional in education.

What was argued at the Brown v Board of Education case?

The NAACP's *(p.39)* argument was that even if equal educational provision and facilities were made available, the Plessy v Ferguson decision from 1896 of 'separate but equal' made black children feel inferior and this therefore broke the 14th Amendment.

What was the 14th Amendment in the US constitution that was important in Brown v Board of Education?

The 14th Amendment to the US constitution gave citizenship to African Americans, which meant they had equal rights and protection under the law.

What was the verdict in the Brown v Board of Education case?

There were 2 main details from the Supreme Court's verdict:

- The Supreme Court ruled that Plessy was unconstitutional and schools should desegregate.
- The ending of racial segregation.

What was the problem with the verdict of the Brown v Board of Education case?

Although the Supreme Court ruled desegregation should happen, it didn't say when. This meant schools could avoid complying with the court's decision.

What did the court rule to enforce desegregation in the Brown v Board of Education case?

The following year, in May 1955, the court further ruled all states must make a 'prompt and reasonable start' on desegregation. However, it still failed to give a deadline for when this should happen.

What was the positive effect of the Brown v Board of Education case?

There were 4 main positive effects of the Brown v Board of Education case:

- It raised awareness of the racial inequalities that existed and kick-started the legal battle for civil rights for all.
- It was massive leap forward in civil rights as the Plessy v Ferguson ruling had been successfully challenged, which paved the way for future challenges in other areas.
- The Supreme Court had finally supported the civil rights movement by ruling in its favour.
- Schools did integrate, but very slowly.

What were the negative effects the Brown v Board of Education case?

There were 5 main negative results for African Americans due to the verdict in the Brown v Topeka case:

- Some people wanted to preserve segregation and an organisation called the White Citizens' Council was set up in Mississippi. This grew into a network.
- African American students regularly experienced threats and bullying after the case.
- Many African American teachers either lost their jobs or experienced harassment from white students.
- As a result of the backlash, black schools with good teachers and high levels of achievement closed.
- Race relations in the south became incredibly tense, with increased violence by the KKK *(p.53)*. It is in this context that the murder of Emmett Till *(p.44)* occurred.

DID YOU KNOW?

Southern states strongly resisted the ruling.
Five years after the Supreme Court ordered an end to segregated schools, over 99% of black Southern children still attended separate schools.

EMMETT TILL MURDER, 1955

'The murder of my son has shown me that what happens to any of us, anywhere in the world, had better be the business of us all.' - Mamie Till-Mobley

Who was Emmett Till?
Emmett Till was an African American boy from Chicago who was brutally murdered by two white men in Mississippi.

When did the murder of Emmett Till happen?
Emmett Till was murdered on 28th August, 1955.

Where did the murder of Emmett Till happen?
The murder took place in Drew, Mississippi, around 30 miles away from Money, Mississippi.

How old was Emmett Till when he was murdered?
Emmett Till was 14 years old when he was murdered.

Why was Emmett Till murdered?
It is not clear exactly what happened in the shop. The 2 main theories are:

- ✅ Emmett Till wolf-whistled at the white shop keeper, Carolyn Bryant.
- ✅ Emmett Till was accused of 'talking inappropriately' to Carolyn Bryant, saying: 'Bye, baby' to her.

What happened to Emmett Till before and when he was murdered?

There were 6 key events around Emmett Till's murder:

- ✅ Emmett Till was from Chicago and arrived in Money, Mississippi on 21st August, 1955. He was visiting his great uncle, Moses Wright.
- ✅ He visited Bryant's Grocery and Meat Market with some friends to buy sweets on 24th August.
- ✅ Emmett might have either wolf-whistled at or spoken to the white shopkeeper, Carolyn Bryant, in a way considered inappropriate at that time.
- ✅ At 2.30am on 28th August, Roy Bryant and his half-brother, J W Milan, kidnapped Emmett. They took him at gunpoint from his great uncle Moses' house.
- ✅ Emmett was driven to a farm in Drew, Mississippi, where he was brutally beaten and then driven to the Tallahatchie River and shot.
- ✅ The killers then disposed of Emmett's body in the Tallahatchie River. His body was found on 31st August.

Who murdered Emmett Till?

Emmett Till was murdered by Roy Bryant, the shopkeeper's husband, and J W Milam, Bryant's half-brother.

What happened after Emmett Till was murdered?

There were 3 key events after Emmett Till's body was found:

- ✅ His mother, Mamie Till, insisted on his body being returned to Chicago and an open-casket funeral was held which thousands of people attended.
- ✅ His murder was reported worldwide and resulted in a huge outcry at the treatment of African Americans in the USA.
- ✅ On 19th September, the murder trial of Roy Bryant and J W Milam began.

What happened to the people who murdered Emmett Till?

There were 4 main events connected to the murderers:

- ✅ Roy Bryant and J W Milan were arrested in September 1955.
- ✅ There was a short trial.
- ✅ The NAACP *(p.39)* protected Emmett Till's great uncle, Moses Wright, as he was a witness at the trial and had received death threats from the KKK *(p.53)*.
- ✅ They were found not guilty by an all-white jury on 23rd September.

What caused outrage about the murder of Emmett Till?

Emmett Till's murder caused outrage for 3 main reasons:

- ✅ Although it was not unusual for an African American boy to be murdered in Mississippi, the killing caused outrage among both the African American and white communities in the north.
- ✅ The fact that the two accused men, Roy Bryant and J W Milam, were found not guilty caused outrage across the world.
- ✅ It demonstrated that African Americans could not get justice in America because of the prejudice of all-male and all-white juries and judges.

Why did the murder of Emmett Till have such importance?

There were 4 main reasons the murder of Emmett Till was important:

- ✅ The growth of the civil rights movement was fuelled by the murder of Emmett Till.

- ☑ For the first time, many white Americans saw the extreme racism faced by African Americans living in the south.
- ☑ More African Americans were encouraged to take part in civil rights protests and bring about change.
- ☑ The murder inspired Rosa Parks to refuse to move on the bus in Montgomery in December 1955.

> **DID YOU KNOW?**
>
> In 2018, the FBI reopened the investigation into Till's murder.

MONTGOMERY BUS BOYCOTT, 1955-56

'Each person must live their life as a model for others.' - Rosa Parks

What was the Montgomery Bus Boycott?

As part of the civil rights protests, African Americans refused to ride on the city buses in Montgomery, Alabama, to show their opposition to segregated seating. Lasting over a year, it became known as the Montgomery Bus Boycott and is regarded as the first large-scale anti-segregation demonstration in the USA.

When was the Montgomery Bus Boycott?

The Montgomery Bus Boycott lasted from 5th December, 1955, to 20th December, 1956.

What caused the Montgomery Bus Boycott?

There were 4 main reasons for the Montgomery Bus Boycott:

- ☑ Buses were segregated in the southern states of America. This was a violation of the constitution's 14th Amendment.
- ☑ On 1st December, 1955, Rosa Parks was instructed by a white bus driver to move out of her seat in the black section of the bus to allow a white man to sit, as the white seating area was full. She refused and was arrested.
- ☑ Although she wasn't the first to refuse to give up her seat, Rosa was a member of the NAACP *(p.39)* and a well-respected citizen. For this reason, she was chosen as the boycott's figurehead.
- ☑ A boycott was called by the Women's Political Council, WPC.

What happened during the Montgomery Bus Boycott?

There were 8 key events during the Montgomery Bus Boycott:

- ☑ The Montgomery Improvement Association (MIA) was created on 1st December in response to Rosa Parks' arrest. The MIA's chairman was Martin Luther King.
- ☑ The boycott started on 5th December, 1955 - the day of Rosa Parks' trial.
- ☑ The bus operator held talks with the leaders of the MIA to discuss what they wanted, but the bus operator refused to desegregate the buses.
- ☑ The MIA organised car-shares and taxi rides for the African Americans so they could get to work during the boycott.
- ☑ The NAACP *(p.39)* brought a court case, Browder versus Gayle, against the bus company on 1st February, 1956.
- ☑ Martin Luther King and others were arrested and fined because of the boycott.
- ☑ The outcome of the Browder versus Gayle case was that buses should be desegregated. The case was taken to the Supreme Court by the bus operator and White Citizens' Councils.
- ☑ The boycott ended on 19th December, 1956, after 381 days. This was following the Supreme Court decision that segregation was unconstitutional and buses should be desegregated.

What was the impact of the Montgomery Bus Boycott?

The majority of African Americans who used the city buses stopped doing so in protest against the segregation rules - around 90% took part in the boycott.

Why did the Montgomery Bus Boycott end?

The NAACP *(p.39)* went to the Supreme Court, claiming bus segregation rules broke the 14th Amendment of the US Constitution. The case was known as Browder v Gayle. The court agreed, and the boycott was ended.

What was the result of the Montgomery Bus Boycott?

There were 2 main results:

- There were two appeals against the decision, but the Supreme Court upheld the ruling that the Montgomery buses should be desegregated.
- On 20th December, African Americans started using the Montgomery buses again.

How was Rosa Parks involved in the Montgomery Bus Boycott?

When the bus driver told Rosa Parks, a civil rights activist, and others to give up their seats for a white man, she refused. As a result, she was arrested.

What was the role of the WPC (Women's Political Council) in the Montgomery Bus Boycott?

The Women's Political Council, or WPC, had campaigned against segregation on buses for years. It had warned the mayor a boycott would take place if one more black person was arrested for breaking bus segregation rules. The bus boycott on 5th December was suggested by the WPC.

What was the role of the churches in the Montgomery Bus Boycott?

During the Montgomery Bus Boycott, the churches in Montgomery played an important role in 3 main ways:

- Churches and church halls were a place for people to gather to organise the boycott.
- Churches raised money to provide support for those involved in the boycott, such as cars for those who were car-sharing.
- Churches raised awareness of the boycott.

What was the role of the MIA during the Montgomery Bus Boycott?

The Montgomery Improvement Association, or MIA, was an organisation formed to support the boycott. As part of this, a car pool system was introduced to provide lifts and transport to those refusing to use the buses.

Who was the leader of the MIA during the Montgomery Bus Boycott?

A respected, educated and peace-loving clergyman, Martin Luther King, became the leader of MIA.

Who opposed the MIA during the Montgomery Bus Boycott?

The White Citizens' Councils and the Ku Klux Klan *(p.53)* strongly opposed the MIA and its activities.

What were the actions of the opposition towards the MIA during the Montgomery Bus Boycott?

There were 4 main ways in which people opposed the actions of the MIA:

- A number of churches and Martin Luther King's *(p.52)* own house were bombed.
- Some people involved in the boycott lost their jobs.
- Boycotters were arrested.

- African Americans were threatened and harrassed.

What was the significance of the Montgomery Bus Boycott?

The Montgomery Bus Boycott was significant for 4 main reasons:

- The boycott raised Martin Luther King's *(p.52)* profile and he became famous nationwide, not just in Alabama.
- The actions of those in Montgomery inspired similar boycotts in other cities. In Tallahassee, Florida, for example, a boycott was held from 28th May to 22nd December, 1956.
- The violent reaction to the boycott and to desegregation by white people showed them in a negative way. This was later used by activists during subsequent protests.
- It demonstrated the importance of media attention in direct, non-violent forms of protest to gain support for the civil rights movement.

What were the negative consequences of the Montgomery Bus Boycott?

There were 2 main negative consequences of the Montgomery Bus Boycott:

- Although the boycott was successful in ending segregation on the buses, this was not extended to other facilities in Montgomery.
- There was an increase in violence by and membership of the KKK *(p.53)*. The buses even had to be stopped until the violence lessened.

> **DID YOU KNOW?**
>
> **Rosa Parks was not the first woman to refuse to give up her seat.**
>
> Nine months before Rosa Parks was arrested, Claudette Colvin was arrested in Montgomery for refusing to give up her seat. However, because she was an unmarried, pregnant teenager, the civil rights movement decided not to publicise her case.

LITTLE ROCK HIGH SCHOOL, 1957

'It's been an interesting year... I've had a course in human relations firsthand.' - Ernest Green of the Little Rock Nine

What was Little Rock High School?

Little Rock was a high school in Arkansas that desegregated. Although 25 African American students were accepted at the school, the threats and violence levelled at them meant only nine attended.

When did the incident at Little Rock High School take place?

The incident at Little Rock High School happened in September 1957.

Why did the incident at Little Rock High School take place?

There are 4 main reasons for the incident at Little Rock High School:

- In the Brown versus the Board of Education of Topeka case of 1954, the Supreme Court had ruled 'separate but equal' in education was unconstitutional and therefore all schools had to integrate.
- In 1957, Little Rock High School was instructed to desegregate by the Federal Court.

- 25 students were chosen out of those that applied to the school, but due to threats from the white community only 9 students tried to attend in September 1957.
- The Governor of Arkansas, Orval Faubus, deliberately tried to stop the 9 black American students from going to Little Rock and there were massive protests by the white community.

What happened at Little Rock High School?

There were 6 main events during the Little Rock High School incident:

- The Arkansas state troops were ordered by Governor Faubus to stop the 9 African American students from entering the school 'to protect them'.
- A massive group of white protesters had gathered, shouting abuse and threats.
- The NAACP (p.39) wanted the 9 African American students to travel together for protection, but Elizabeth Eckford did not get the message and arrived alone.
- Elizabeth Eckford faced the angry mob and was prevented from entering the school by state troops. The media covered the incident and there was an outcry.
- President Eisenhower now intervened by issuing a presidential order that removed the state troops and sent in federal troops to escort the 9 students to school.
- Federal troops protected the 9 students for a whole school year.

What was the reaction to the incident at Little Rock High School?

Pictures and reports were shared across the USA and in other countries, with some 250 reporters relating events. The news caused outrage in America and beyond.

What did the NAACP do to help the students in Little Rock High School?

The group of African American students were advised by the NAACP (p.39) to meet and walk to school together supervised by ministers.

What went wrong on the first day of school in Little Rock High School?

One of the students, Elizabeth Eckford, did not receive the message from the NAACP (p.39) and went to Little Rock High School alone as planned. She arrived alone to find a waiting mob, who yelled insults and called for her to be lynched.

What did the governor do to stop desegregation in Little Rock High School?

Governor Orval Faubus of Arkansas took 4 main actions to stop integration:

- He arranged huge protests against desegregation outside the school gates.
- He also ordered 250 state troops to stop the African American students from entering.
- He ignored President Eisenhower's request to desegregate the school when they met on 12th September, 1957.
- He closed all schools in the state to avoid integrating them in September 1958.

What were the loopholes used by state governments to avoid desegregation after the incident at Little Rock High School?

The Arkansas state government used the following 6 loopholes to avoid desegregation:

- The following school year, 1958 to 1959, Faubus closed every school in Little Rock to stop integration happening.
- Just one school year at a time was desegregated.
- Only a few African American pupils were accepted into each school.
- A few schools in a given area were desegregated to comply with the law, but segregation remained in force at the rest.
- Testing methods were introduced that were rigged against African American students being successful.
- At some schools, protests and riots were used as an excuse to keep African American students from attending, saying it was for the children's own protection.

Get our free app at GCSEHistory.com

What was the significance of the incident at Little Rock High School?

The incident at Little Rock was significant for 5 main reasons:

- The president's role was important. President Eisenhower intervened to support integration despite the fact he was personally opposed to desegregation being enforced.
- Although 'state' rights' existed, a state could be overruled by the federal government to uphold Supreme Court decisions.
- The media had a massive impact on public opinion. America and the world were horrified by the violence used by white protesters against the 9 students and some black American reporters.
- This made civil rights activists realised the importance of gaining media attention in future campaigns as a means to put pressure on the federal government to support change.
- It was announced that massive resistance to desegregation would be illegal.

DID YOU KNOW?

The Little Rock Nine suffered harassment and racism at school.
Minnijean Brown was expelled because she called two girls 'white trash' after they targeted her.

BUSSING

'Effective but never popular.' - Washington Post

What was bussing?

To force desegregation, bussing was used. This involved using buses to transport children from black areas to a white area to go to school, or vice versa.

Why did people not like bussing?

People objected because they did not want their children to attend a mixed-race school or have to travel across town.

How did people avoid bussing?

Some white parents moved away from urban areas to avoid their children having to be educated alongside black children.

DID YOU KNOW?

Since bussing stopped in 1999, schools have become more segregated.
In 2016, 60% of black American students were attending schools with less than 10% white Americans.

CIVIL RIGHTS ACT, 1957

'The final battle against intolerance is to be fought - not in the chambers of any legislature - but in the hearts of men.' - President Dwight Eisenhower, 1956

What was the Civil Rights Act of 1957?
The Civil Rights Act of 1957 allowed the government to prosecute states who interfered with people's right to vote.

When was the 1957 Civil Rights Act made into law?
It became law on 9th September, 1957.

Who signed the 1957 Civil Rights Act?
President Dwight D Eisenhower signed the act into law.

Why was the 1957 Civil Rights Act created?
There are 2 main reasons why the Civil Rights Act of 1957 was introduced:

- President Eisenhower supported the act because of the success of both the civil rights movement and the Montgomery Bus Boycott *(p.46)*. However, President Eisenhower was unwilling to fully support civil rights.
- The success of these events put President Eisenhower under more pressure to introduce the act.

What did the 1957 Civil Rights Act introduce?
The Civil Rights Act of 1957 introduced 2 main changes:

- It set up a federal Civil Rights Commission which could investigate racial discrimination.
- It set up a system whereby the federal government could prosecute states that interfered with people's right to vote.

What were the limitations of the 1957 Civil Rights Act?
The Civil Rights Act of 1957 was limited in 3 main ways:

- Court cases were unlikely to find in favour of African Americans due to racism - the majority of judges and jury members were white. The Dixiecrats *(p.54)* amended the bill to include juries in the court cases rather than just using judges.
- Dixiecrats *(p.54)* forced the bill to be amended to weaken the federal government's ability to interfere with individual state laws.
- Due to the limitations of the law, its impact was diminished.

What was the impact of the 1957 Civil Rights Act?
The Civil Rights Act of 1957 had 3 main consequences:

- It was the first time the federal government had brought in civil rights legislation for 82 years, which was a major step forward for the civil rights movement.
- Civil rights organisations and protesters were frustrated by the limitations of the act and were determined to step up campaigning for greater change.
- It could be seen as the stepping stone to the Civil Rights Act of 1960.

DID YOU KNOW?

In the 1956 presidential campaign neither Eisenhower nor his Democratic opponent, Stevenson, paid much attention to civil rights.

MARTIN LUTHER KING

'The ultimate measure of a man is not where he stands in moments of comfort and convenience, but where he stands at times of challenge and controversy.' - Martin Luther King

Who was Martin Luther King?
Martin Luther King was an African American who became one of the world's most famous civil rights campaigners. In 1964 he won the Nobel Peace Prize.

What did Martin Luther King do before he campaigned for civil rights?
Martin Luther King Junior was born into a middle-class family in 1929. He was a Baptist minister and gained a doctorate at university.

Why did Martin Luther King gain widespread support?
He had 2 main qualities that meant he appealed to everyone:
- He was well educated, a passionate speaker and continually emphasised his non-violent stance.
- Most importantly, he was a Baptist minister which meant he had the respect of many people.

Why was Martin Luther King committed to a non-violent approach?
He was influenced by the teachings of Mahatma Gandhi who led India's battle for independence using a non-violent approach. He was also a committed Christian, following Jesus's message of non-violence.

What did Martin Luther King want the civil rights movement to achieve?
Initially, Martin Luther King was focused on 2 main areas:
- Ending segregation in the southern states of America.
- Increasing voter registration in the south's black communities so they had more political power.

How did Martin Luther King's aims change?
Martin Luther King focus switched to 2 different priorities after 1965:
- Tackling economic and social inequalities across America to address the issues black Americans faced in terms of jobs, housing and wages.
- Opposing the Vietnam War *(p.91)* which diverted resources from solving social and racial problems at home.

What events in the civil right movement did Martin Luther King organise?
Martin Luther King was involved in many events. The 5 main events included:
- The creation of the Southern Christian Leadership Conference in 1955.
- The Montgomery Bus Boycott *(p.46)*, 1955.
- Campaign C *(p.59)* in Birmingham, Alabama, 1963.
- The March on Washington *(p.61)* in August 1963.
- The Selma to Montgomery March in March 1965.

What was important about Martin Luther King?
Martin Luther King is one of the most important figures in 20th century American history due to his tireless campaigning for civil rights. His significance in America has led to many roads and schools being named after him and there is even an annual public holiday in his honour.

How did Martin Luther King die?
Martin Luther King was assassinated in Memphis, Tennessee on 4th April, 1968.

> **DID YOU KNOW?**
> Time Magazine made King its 'Man of the Year' for 1963.

OPPOSITION TO CIVIL RIGHTS
'I say segregation now, segregation tomorrow, segregation forever.' - Governor George Wallace

Who opposed the civil rights movement?
Opposition to the civil rights movement came from all parts of society, including the Ku Klux Klan *(p.53)* in the Deep South and the so-called Dixiecrats *(p.54)* in Congress.

> **DID YOU KNOW?**
> There were several groups which opposed civil rights:
> - The Ku Klux Klan is arguably the most famous.
> - White Citizens' Councils were formed after the Brown v Board of Education case.

KU KLUX KLAN
'Literally half the town belonged to the Klan when I was a boy.' - Robert Coughlan

What was the Ku Klux Klan?
The Ku Klux Klan, or KKK, was a white supremacist organisation that aimed to ensure white people continued to have more rights than, and power over, other races. Its members dressed in white robes and hoods.

What was the history of the Ku Klux Klan?
The Ku Klux Klan existed for many years before the First World War, but its power grew after the conflict.
- It was formed in the 1860s, after the American Civil War.
- Its actions were restricted by the government in 1871 through the Ku Klux Klan Act, but it continued as an underground movement.
- Insurance salesman William Simmonds restarted the organisation in 1915 after being inspired by the film, 'Birth Of A Nation'.
- At its height, in 1925, it had 5 million members.

Who were the members of the Ku Klux Klan?

Most KKK members were white churchgoers from southern areas of America who were regarded as respected members of society.

What did the Ku Klux Klan believe in?

The Ku Klux Klan expanded its beliefs after the First World War.

- They believed WASPs - White Anglo-Saxon Protestants - should fight for survival and dominance over other races.
- They believed immigration threatened WASPs and should be stopped.
- They enforced some traditional Christian values by attacking people of other religions and groups they saw as 'immoral', such as divorcees.
- They claimed segregation was supported by the words of the Bible.

How was the Ku Klux Klan organised?

When William Simmonds set up the new KKK, he increased its appeal by making it more like an exclusive club with a mysterious code.

- The Klan was divided into chapters, or local groups, called Klaverns.
- There were different levels of authority in the Klan. Klaverns were led by Kleagles, who answered to Klugs. The overall leader was called the Imperial Wizard.
- The Klan's rules were written in a book called the Kloran.

What did the Ku Klux Klan do?

The KKK used several methods to intimidate and persecute anyone it felt was a threat to WASP supremacy, including black people, immigrants and critics.

- Its members intimidated people. Sometimes they would burn crosses outside their victims' homes to denote them as a target.
- The Klan used violence and members were often involved in lynchings. They also beat, burned, and tarred and feathered their victims.
- Its members protested against politicians with whom it disagreed and influenced lawmaking where possible.
- Members boycotted any businesses owned by those who disagreed with them.

DID YOU KNOW?

In the early 1920s, there were around 50 lynchings a year.

DIXIECRATS

'There's not enough troops in the army to force the southern people to break down segregation...' - Strom Thurmond

Who were the Dixiecrats?

The Dixiecrats was another name for the States' Rights Democratic Party, a political party set up in the Deep South because it supported segregation. The name 'Dixiecrats' was also used for southern conservative Democrats.

When were the Dixiecrats created?
The Dixiecrats, or States' Rights Democratic Party, was set up in 1948; it was also dissolved in the same year.

Why were the Dixiecrats created?
The Dixiecrats, or States' Rights Democratic Party, was set up by its members because they opposed President Truman's Executive Order 9918, which ended racial discrimination in the US armed forces.

How did the Dixiecrats oppose the Civil Rights Acts?
They would filibuster, a tactic used in Congress to prevent a vote on a bill. The most common filibuster was to talk until the time limit on debate was reached.

Who were the members of the Dixiecrats?
The Dixiecrats were former Democrats.

> **DID YOU KNOW?**
>
> **South Carolina's Strom Thurmond broke the filibuster record.**
> He held the floor for just over 24 continuous hours to prevent the 1964 Civil Rights Act from passing through Congress.

SIT-INS, 1960

'And I had had enough. And I made up my mind that I had to do something.' - Joseph McNeil, one of the Greensboro Four

What was the Greensboro Sit-In?
The Greensboro Sit-In was a protest against segregation at a lunch counter in Greensboro, North Carolina.

When was the Greensboro Sit-in?
The Greensboro Sit-In started on 1st February, 1960.

Why did the Greensboro Sit-in happen?
There were 2 main reasons:
- The students who were involved were inspired by the Montgomery Bus Boycott *(p.46)*, the Freedom Riders, and non-violent civil rights protests. They were also deeply affected by the murder of Emmett Till *(p.44)*.
- They wanted to end the segregation of the lunch-counters.

What happened during the Greensboro Sit-In?
There were 5 main events during the Greensboro Sit-In:
- Four male students from a local agricultural and technical college entered a Woolworth's store and sat at the whites-only lunch counter.
- They were asked to leave and the police were called when they refused.
- The police were not able to arrest them as they had not broken a law.

- ✓ The media was there to cover the story in the news.
- ✓ The students sat in their seats until the store closed.

What were the reactions to the Greensboro Sit-in?

There were 5 main reactions to the Greensboro Sit-In.

- ✓ The next day, the same students took 25 others with them and sat at the lunch counter.
- ✓ More students were inspired to join the protest, and within three days there were 300 students staging sit-ins at other locations. In a month, there were sit-ins in 54 cities across 7 states. By April, more than 50,000 people were involved.
- ✓ A non-violent student group, the Student Nonviolent Coordinating Committee (SNCC *(p.56)*), was set up to train students to carry out sit-ins peacefully in April 1960.
- ✓ The media was mostly supportive of what was happening and white people began to join in the protests.
- ✓ Lunch counters around the south started to desegregate by the summer of 1960. The Woolworth's lunch counter desegregated on 25th July that year.

Why was the Greensboro Sit-in significant?

The sit-ins were significant for 4 main reasons:

- ✓ Young people and white people joined the protest.
- ✓ While the protest was still a form of non-violent direct action, it was hard to ignore.
- ✓ They attracted a lot of media attention.
- ✓ The sit-ins led to similar protests around the country such as prayer-ins at segregated churches and wade-ins at segregated swimming pools.

DID YOU KNOW?

Joseph McNeil achieved a degree in engineering physics.
He went on to join the US Air Force.

STUDENT NONVIOLENT COORDINATING COMMITTEE

'Unlike mainstream civil rights groups, which merely sought integration of blacks into the existing order, SNCC sought structural changes in American society itself.' - Julian Bond

What was the Student Nonviolent Coordinating Committee?

The Student Nonviolent Coordinating Committee, or SNCC, was a student group involved in the civil rights movement. SNCC was pronounced 'snick'.

When was the Student Nonviolent Coordinating Committee created?

The Student Nonviolent Coordinating Committee was created in April 1960 and was closed down by 1970.

Who set up the Student Nonviolent Coordinating Committee?

The Student Nonviolent Coordinating Committee was set up by students with the help of Ella Baker, a member of the SCLC *(p.41)*.

Where was the Student Nonviolent Coordinating Committee created?
The Student Nonviolent Coordinating Committee was set up at Shaw University in Rayleigh, in the state of North Carolina.

Why was the Student Nonviolent Coordinating Committee created?
The Student Nonviolent Coordinating Committee was set up in response to the sit-ins in Greensboro to enable black and white students to work together in the civil rights movement.

What did the Student Nonviolent Coordinating Committee do?
The Student Nonviolent Coordinating Committee was involved in 6 main events:
- Sit-ins, such as the ones in Greensboro.
- Freedom Riders in 1961.
- The March on Washington *(p.61)*, 1963.
- Freedom Summer *(p.62)* in 1964.
- Selma to Montgomery March, 1965.
- March against Fear in 1966.

How did Stokely Carmichael change the Student Nonviolent Coordinating Committee?
The Student Nonviolent Coordinating Committee changed in 4 main ways under the leadership of Stokely Carmichael:
- He became the leader of SNCC in 1966 and made SNCC a blacks-only organisation.
- He rejected the non-violent, peaceful campaign tactics.
- He coined the phrase 'black power' during the March Against Fear in 1966, which inspired the movement of the same name.
- He left SNCC in 1967.

DID YOU KNOW?

Stokely Carmichael joined SNCC in 1961.
He was a Freedom Rider.

FREEDOM RIDERS, 1961

'When growing up, I saw segregation. I saw racial discrimination.' - John Lewis, one of the original Freedom Riders

Who were the Freedom Riders?
The Freedom Riders were white and black American civil rights activists who took bus journeys across different states to protest against segregation on transport.

When did the Freedom Riders ride the buses?
The Freedom Riders were active between 4th May and 10th December, 1961.

Where did the Freedom Riders ride the buses?

There were 5 main states where they rode buses:

- Louisiana.
- Mississippi.
- Alabama.
- Georgia.
- South Carolina.

Who organised the Freedom Riders?

The Freedom Riders were organised by CORE *(p.40)* and SNCC *(p.56)* members.

Why did the Freedom Riders take bus rides into the Deep South?

To challenge and draw attention to the non-enforcement of a Supreme Court ruling that stated all transport and facilities should be desegregated.

What happened to the Freedom Riders at Anniston?

There were 4 main events at Anniston:

- The Freedom Riders faced an angry mob of white protesters who attacked the bus. A police escort led the bus away from the city but the mob followed. The driver was forced to pull over as the tyres were damaged.
- The mob attacked the bus and a firebomb was thrown through one of the smashed windows. The passengers were able to escape when highway patrolmen arrived to prevent more attacks.
- A second bus was also attacked when it arrived in Anniston, and its passengers beaten up.
- Eventually, the bus finished its journey in Montgomery. Bull Connor, the police chief, allowed KKK *(p.53)* members to attack the passengers.

What results did the Freedom Riders' trips have?

The Freedom Riders' activities had 3 main outcomes:

- Buses were attacked by Ku Klux Klan *(p.53)* members and riders were beaten up.
- Over 300 riders were sent to jail in Jackson, Mississippi.
- There were over 60 freedom rides during the summer of 1961.

What were the consequences of the Freedom Riders' actions?

There were 3 main consequences to the rides and retaliations:

- State police and politicians had supported the KKK *(p.53)*, so the actions of its members were a huge embarrassment for the government.
- President Kennedy *(p.80)* intervened by announcing federal officers would be deployed to enforce the desegregation ruling.
- The southern states therefore took action to desegregate buses and facilities.

DID YOU KNOW?

John Lewis, one of the original 13 Freedom Riders, was elected to the House of Representatives in 1986.

He received the Presidential Medal of Freedom in 2011.

JAMES MEREDITH CASE, 1961

'I can't fight alone.' - James Meredith, 1963

What was the James Meredith case?
In 1961, the University of Mississippi rejected James Meredith as a student. The following year, the Supreme Court ordered he should be admitted after the NAACP *(p.39)* successfully argued he had been rejected because he was black.

Who was James Meredith in the famous Supreme Court case?
James Meredith was an African American who was refused a place at Mississippi University.

How did the Mississippi government react to the James Meredith case?
Both the state government *(p.16)* and university officials ignored the court ruling and instead physically prevented James Meredith from registering as a student.

How did the federal government try to help after the James Meredith case?
The federal government tried to help in 2 ways:
- ☑ James Meredith was protected by 500 federal officials while he registered.
- ☑ President John F Kennedy made appeals for calm on television and radio.

What happened when James tried to register after the James Meredith case?
A 3,000-strong mob attacked the federal officials and shot 28 of them. Two civilians died and a further 375 were injured as a result of the riots.

How did the riots caused by the James Meredith case end?
Federal troops were sent in to bring a halt to the disruption and also assigned to protect James Meredith for the whole year.

Why was the James Meredith case significant?
It forced the President to enforce a Supreme Court ruling, which meant black students were rarely stopped from attending integrated universities.

> **DID YOU KNOW?**
>
> In 1966, James Meredith wrote the book, Three Years in Mississippi, about his time at Mississippi University.

CAMPAIGN C, 1963

'... give our community a chance to survive.' - Fred Shuttlesworth, 1963

What was the Campaign C?
The aim of Campaign C was to end segregation by provoking white violence to gain support for civil rights legislation. The 'C' stood for confrontation.

When did Campaign C occur?
Campaign C happened in April and May, 1963.

Where was Campaign C held?
Campaign C took place in Birmingham, Alabama.

Why did the campaigners choose Birmingham for Campaign C?
Birmingham was chosen for 3 key reasons:
- ✅ It had not desegregated any facilities.
- ✅ Its police chief, Bull Connor, was also well known for using violence against African Americans. He had failed to stop the KKK *(p.53)* attacking the Freedom Riders in 1961.
- ✅ Birmingham was nicknamed 'Bombingham' because of its reputation for violence against African Americans. It was hoped the civil rights campaign would result in a reaction from the white community and gain media attention.

Who was involved in Campaign C?
There were 3 key groups involved:
- ✅ The SNCC *(p.56)*.
- ✅ The SCLC *(p.41)* and Martin Luther King.
- ✅ The Alabama Christian Movement for Human Rights (ACMHR).

What methods were used for Campaign C?
The campaign's methods included sit-ins, boycotts, peaceful marches and the training of young demonstrators, as most of the adults were in jail.

What happened during Campaign C?
There were 5 important events during Campaign C:
- ✅ A march which resulted in mass arrests on 3rd April, 1963.
- ✅ The organisers trained children in non-violent methods.
- ✅ On 2nd May, the children marched during the Children's Crusade; 956 of them were arrested and put in jail.
- ✅ On 3rd May, more children marched and the police used police dogs and fire hoses on them. Their actions were caught on camera and shown across the nation.
- ✅ President Kennedy *(p.80)* intervened as rioting took place and sent federal troops to Birmingham on 12th May.

What happened during the first protest of Campaign C?
The first march began on 3rd April. Many protesters were arrested, including Martin Luther King.

What happened during the children's marches in Campaign C?
On 2nd May, a children's march took place involving around 1,000 young people. There was another children's march the following day, and this time the police used dogs and powerful water hoses in response.

What were the results of Campaign C?
There were 5 main consequences of the campaign:
- ✅ On 10th May the senior citizens' committee, responsible for many of Birmingham's businesses, desegregated its lunch counters and allowed African Americans to be employed.

- Over 200 journalists and photographers captured the police brutality. Media reports horrified the nation and the world, and people felt sympathy for the protesters.
- This led to President Kennedy's *(p.80)* intervention in support of the civil rights movement. He addressed the nation, promising he would 'ask Congress to act, to make a commitment it has not fully made in this century to the proposition that race has no place in American life or laws'.
- It created the momentum needed for the organisation of the March on Washington *(p.61)* in August 1963.
- There was an increase in KKK *(p.53)* attacks and NAACP *(p.39)* leader, Medgar Evers, was murdered in June 1963.

> **DID YOU KNOW?**
>
> One estimate says there were 50 bombings in Birmingham, Alabama, between 1947 and 1965.

WASHINGTON MARCH, 1963

'I have a dream.' - Martin Luther King at the March on Washington

What was the March on Washington in 1963?

The March on Washington was the largest political protest in US history to campaign for the civil and economic rights of African Americans. The full name of the event was the March on Washington for Jobs and Freedom.

When did the March on Washington take place?

The March on Washington was on 28th August, 1963.

Who organised the March on Washington?

There were 5 main civil rights and religious groups involved with organising the March on Washington:
- NAACP *(p.39)*.
- CORE *(p.40)*.
- SCLC *(p.41)*.
- American Jewish Congress.
- SNCC *(p.56)*.

Who took part in the March on Washington?

Estimates put the number of people who took part in the March on Washington at between 250,000 and 500,000. Around 40,000 of them were white.

Why was the March on Washington organised?

There were 3 main reasons for the March on Washington:
- The civil rights movement wanted to build on the momentum created by Campaign C *(p.59)* in Birmingham, Alabama.
- The KKK's *(p.53)* opposition to the civil rights movement had grown so African Americans and civil right activists faced increasing danger.
- Despite President Kennedy *(p.80)* publicly supporting civil rights and a civil rights bill, nothing had been passed by the government, so they wanted to increase pressure on the government to make changes.

What happened at the March on Washington?

There were 3 main events at the March on Washington:

- Black and white civil rights protesters from all over America travelled to Washington.
- The event was one of the first to be broadcast around the world.
- There were speeches and music, and Martin Luther King gave the closing speech called 'I have a dream'.

What happened as a result of the March on Washington?

The March on Washington had 5 main consequences:

- It widened the divide in the civil rights movement between those who non-violent protests and integration was the way forward and those who felt the aims were not radical enough. For example, Malcolm X *(p.68)* called the march, 'the farce on Washington'.
- President Kennedy *(p.80)* met with the key civil rights leaders and, after the march, gave greater support to passing a civil rights bill.
- However, no civil rights bill was passed until 1964.
- There was an increase in violent opposition to the civil rights movement. For example, a church was bombed in Birmingham 14 days after the march, resulting in the deaths of 4 black American girls.
- The civil rights movement received even more support.

Why was the March on Washington so important?

There were 4 main reasons why the March on Washington was important:

- It was the largest political protest in US history.
- It was a peaceful protest and was broadcast around the world. Famous high-profile people such as singer Bob Dylan and actor Marlon Brando were visibly involved.
- Martin Luther King's *(p.52)* closing speech, 'I have a dream', confirmed his role as a civil rights leader and showed how important the issue had become.
- It brought huge publicity to the cause and was supported by many people, both black and white.

DID YOU KNOW?

The March on Washington was televised.
CBS provided live coverage in America and six other countries followed the march as it happened.

FREEDOM SUMMER, 1964

'This will be a real turning point in terms of whether it will be possible to get anything out of the political structures that is meaningful in this country.' - Robert Moses, 1964

What was Freedom Summer?

Freedom Summer was a project aimed at increasing the number of registered black American voters in the state of Mississippi. It was called the Mississippi Summer Project.

When did Freedom Summer occur?

Freedom Summer happened between June and August, 1964.

What was the purpose of Freedom Summer?

There were 4 main reasons for Freedom Summer:

- To increase voter registration as it was an election year.
- To provide other community projects, such as summer schools.
- To target Mississippi, which had the lowest percentage of African American voters registered to vote even though 45% of its population was black. It was one of the most segregated states in the USA.
- To help African Americans pass the difficult literacy test so they could register to vote.

Who organised Freedom Summer?

Freedom Summer was organised by 2 groups:

- SNCC (p.56).
- CORE (p.40).

What happened during Freedom Summer?

There were 5 main events during Freedom Summer:

- More than 700 volunteers, mostly white and from middle-class backgrounds, joined African Americans in Mississippi to work on projects in black communities.
- They trained African Americans how to pass the literacy tests and set up 'Freedom Schools' which taught subjects like maths and black history.
- The project was targeted by the KKK (p.53).
- On 21st June 3 CORE (p.40) activists, Michael Schwerner, James Chaney and Andrew Goodman, were arrested, released by the police and went missing.
- On 4th August, their bodies were discovered. They had been murdered.

What opposition was there to Freedom Summer?

There were 2 main forms of opposition to Freedom Summer:

- The volunteers faced huge opposition from the KKK (p.53), which burned down 37 black churches and 30 homes.
- In June 1964, three volunteers - two of them white were abducted and killed by the KKK (p.53). Although 18 men later appeared in court for civil rights violations, none was charged with murder.

Did Freedom Summer work?

There were 5 main consequences of Freedom Summer:

- President Lyndon B Johnson (p.82) was persuaded to pass the Civil Rights Act of 1964, partly due to media coverage of events.
- Only 1,600 out of the 17,000 black people who tried to register to vote were successful.
- The violent reaction by the KKK (p.53) resulted in at least 6 deaths of civil rights workers, 80 physical beatings, over 60 bomb attacks, more than 1000 arrests and 35 shootings.
- It did successfully provide a basic education to many African Americans.
- It was successful in that it raised awareness of voter registration problems.

DID YOU KNOW?

During the Mississippi Freedom Summer, the 32 major projects set up were primarily the work of SNCC and CORE.

MISSISSIPPI MURDERS, 1964

'The FBI is seeking information concerning the disappearance at Philadelphia, Mississippi, of these three individuals...' - FBI poster, 1964

What were the Mississippi Murders?

Three male volunteers were arrested by a policeman who was a Klan *(p.53)* member during the Freedom Summer *(p.62)* project. On their release from prison they disappeared. Their bodies were eventually found.

When did the Mississippi Murders happen?

The Mississippi Murders took place between 21st June and 4th August, 1964.

Who was killed in the Mississippi Murders?

3 civil rights activists were murdered:

- James Chaney.
- Andrew Goodman.
- Michael Schwerner.

What happened during the Mississippi Murders?

There were 6 main incidents during the Mississippi Murders:

- Michael Schwerner, James Chaney and Andrew Goodman were 3 CORE *(p.40)* activists who went to investigate the burning of a Freedom Summer *(p.62)* school.
- They were arrested on 21st June, 1964.
- They were released by the police in the middle of the night and followed by a mob.
- The FBI became involved in the case when Attorney General Robert Kennedy *(p.80)* heard about the incident.
- The activists' bodies were found by FBI agents on 4th August, 1964. They had been shot in the head and Chaney, who was a black American, had been badly beaten.
- An initial court case failed, but in 1967 18 men were charged with violating the victims' civil rights. Just 7 were found guilty and sentenced to between 3 and 10 years in jail. No verdict was reached on 3 of the accused, and 1 was found not guilty as he was a Baptist minister. The remaining cases were dismissed.

What effect did the Mississippi Murders have on the national debate?

The deaths attracted huge publicity and support for civil rights.

DID YOU KNOW?

In 1967, court cases against 18 defendants resulted in just 7 being found guilty of civil rights offences.

Edgar Ray Killen was found not guilty as he was a Baptist minister. He was subsequently convicted of manslaughter in 2005.

CIVIL RIGHTS ACT, 1964

'No memorial oration or eulogy could more eloquently honour President Kennedy's memory than the earliest possible passage of the civil rights bill for which he fought so long.' - President Lyndon B Johnson

What was the Civil Rights Act of 1964?
The Civil Rights Act of 1964 was an important step towards ending discrimination in the USA *(p.37)*.

When was the Civil Rights Act of 1964 passed?
The Civil Rights Act of 1964 was passed on 2nd July, 1964.

Who introduced the Civil Rights Act of 1964?
The Civil Rights Act was introduced by President Kennedy *(p.80)*.

Who passed the Civil Rights Act of 1964?
It was passed by President Johnson *(p.82)*.

Why was the Civil Rights Act of 1964 important?
There were 4 main reasons the Civil Rights Act was important.
- It legally ended segregation.
- It banned discrimination in voter registration tests.
- It banned segregation in public places, such as motels, restaurants and theatres.
- It set up an Equal Opportunities Commission to deal with job discrimination.

How was the Civil Right Act of 1964 successful?
It had 2 main successes:
- It banned segregation in public places.
- The federal government increased its role in ensuring people were accorded their civil rights.

How was the Civil Rights Act of 1964 limited?
There were 4 main limitations to the Civil Rights Act:
- It did not ban discrimination.
- Businesses and schools found ways around desegregation.
- The Equal Opportunities Commission only dealt with complaints, which were rarely made due to those affected being threatened if they did so.
- There was no federal enforcement of the law with regards to voter registration tests.

Who opposed the Civil Rights Act of 1964?
Among opposition to the Civil Rights Act were these 3 key examples:
- The Southern Democrats, nicknamed the 'Dixiecrats *(p.54)*' and some Republicans opposed the new act.
- Some public places tried to get around the law by becoming private businesses.
- There was increased violence towards civil rights activists who attempted to increase voter registration among African Americans.

What did the failures of the Civil Rights Act of 1964 lead to in the Civil Rights Movement?

The failures of the Civil Rights Act of 1964 led to the March from Selma to Montgomery in March 1965.

> **DID YOU KNOW?**
>
> **President John F Kennedy had proposed the Civil Rights Bill but was assassinated before it could be passed.**
>
> He was visiting Dallas, Texas, to gain support for the bill from southern Democrats, or 'Dixiecrats', when he was shot dead.

SELMA, 1964

'Our legs uttered songs. Even without words, our march was worship. I felt my legs were praying.' - Abraham Joshua Heschel

What were the Selma marches?

The Selma to Montgomery marches, organised by civil rights activists, saw protesters march from Selma to Montgomery, Alabama. There were three marches in total, covering 87 kilometres.

When were the Selma marches?

The Selma to Montgomery marches took place between 7th and 25th March, 1965.

Who led the Selma marches?

The 2 main organisers of the Selma to Montgomery marches were:
- ☑ The SCLC *(p.41)* with Martin Luther King.
- ☑ SNCC *(p.56)*.

What was the reason for the Selma marches?

There were 2 main reasons for the Selma to Montgomery marches:
- ☑ To increase the number of African Americans registered to vote; despite Selma having a large black population, just 2% of African Americans were registered.
- ☑ To protest against the unfair registration tests.

What happened during the Selma marches?

There were 6 main events during the Selma to Montgomery marches:
- ☑ On 7th March, 1965, the protesters were stopped by state troopers who attacked them with tear gas and electric cattle prods. The incident, known as Bloody Sunday, was caught on camera.
- ☑ After Bloody Sunday was shown on television, many more people joined the march, including religious leaders and civil rights protesters.
- ☑ The second march, organised by Martin Luther King, set off on 9th March. The marches got as far as Edmund Pettus Bridge on the outskirts of Selma.
- ☑ They were met by state troopers. The marchers knelt in prayer and the troopers moved out of the way. Martin Luther King then called off the march.

- On 15th March, President Johnson *(p.82)* publicly supported the demonstrators and called for Congress to back his voting rights bill.
- President Johnson *(p.82)* used executive orders to put the state national guard under federal control. He ordered them to escort the Selma marchers safely to Montgomery, where they arrived on 25th March, 1965.

What were the consequences of the Selma marches?

Selma had 3 main consequences:

- Footage of African Americans being attacked on what became known as Bloody Sunday was broadcast around the world. This led to an increase in support from President Johnson *(p.82)*.
- President Johnson *(p.82)* used events at Selma to persuade Congress to pass the Voting Rights Act *(p.67)*.
- The violent reaction of the state troopers and those who opposed the civil rights movement led to more a militant style of protest by some sections of the civil rights movement in the years ahead.

> **DID YOU KNOW?**
> SCLC chose Selma because they were impressed with the commitment of local campaigners to the civil rights movement.

VOTING RIGHTS ACT, 1965

'The vote is the most powerful instrument ever devised by man for breaking down injustice.' - President Lyndon B Johnson

What was the Voting Rights Act of 1965?

The Voting Rights Act of 1965 was an important piece of federal legislation that made racial discrimination in voting illegal in the United States.

When was the Voting Rights Act passed?

The Voting Rights Act was passed on 6th August, 1965.

Who passed the Voting Rights Act?

The Voting Rights Act was signed into law by President Lyndon B Johnson *(p.82)*.

Why was the Voting Rights Act of 1965 created?

There were 2 main reasons for the creation of the Voting Rights Act 1965:

- There were still major barriers to African Americans registering to vote as the Civil Rights Act of 1964 was not enforced.
- The march from Selma to Montgomery in March 1965, and the televised violence of Bloody Sunday, put pressure on President Johnson *(p.82)* to act.

What changes did the Voting Rights Act of 1965 introduce?

The Voting Rights Act brought in 3 main changes:

- Every state had to have the same voting registration requirements.
- The literacy tests were made illegal.
- Federal officials would supervise elections in states where voter registration was below 50%.

What consequences were there to the Voting Rights Act of 1965?

Ther Voting Rights Act of 1965 led to 4 main consequences:

- The March Against Fear was organised by James Meredith to encourage African Americans in Mississippi to register to vote. Meredith was shot during the march and Martin Luther King and Stokely Carmichael took his place.
- Almost 80,000 new voters were registered by December 1965, a number which continued to increase.
- Slowly, more African Americans were elected into public office as mayors, senators, and congressmen etc.
- There was frustration the government was not doing enough as the process was so slow.

> **DID YOU KNOW?**
>
> Martin Luther King, John Lewis and Rosa Parks were present when President Johnson signed the Voting Rights Act.

MALCOLM X

'... I see an American nightmare.' - Malcolm X, 1964

Who was Malcolm X?

Malcolm X was a civil rights activist who believed in black nationalism and separatism. Born Malcolm Little in 1925, he was a member of the Nation of Islam.

What was Malcolm X's early life like?

Malcolm X's life was shaped by 4 key events in his early life:

- His father was murdered in a racist attack when he six years old.
- He and his siblings were separated and put into foster care after their mother was committed to a mental institution.
- He was heavily involved in crime.
- He spent time in prison for burglary where he was introduced to the Nation of Islam.

Where did Malcolm X get his name?

Malcolm X stated that the 'X' symbolised the true African family name he could never know. His ancestors were forced to take the name 'Little' by the family that owned them as slaves.

What did Malcolm X believe?

Malcolm X had 3 main beliefs:

- He was critical of the civil rights movement, and leaders like Martin Luther King in particular, because they worked with white people and the government to encourage change.
- He became a voice for those who felt non-violent action had failed. He accepted violence may be necessary, although only in self defence.
- After his split with the Nation of Islam in 1964 and his pilgrimage to Mecca, his beliefs changed. He began to work with white civil rights protesters and talked about human rights.

What was the difference between Malcolm X and Martin Luther King?

Although Malcolm X was still a member of the Nation of Islam, the differences between him and Martin Luther King were clear. There were 4 key differences:

- Malcolm X believed in seperation, whereas Martin Luther King believed in integration.
- Malcolm X focused on the economic, political and social inequalities African Americans faced in the whole of America, whereas Martin Luther King focused on ending segregation and improving voter registration in the south.
- Malcolm X did not believe in working with white people or the government, at least initially, whereas Martin Luther King did.
- Malcolm X did not rule out violent protest if violence was used against African Americans, whereas Martin Luther King advocated peaceful protest.

What was the Nation of Islam Malcolm X was associated with?

There are 4 main things to note about the Nation of Islam:

- It was a black nationalist group created in 1930, and still exists today.
- Members believed in the separation of black and white people, not integration. They believed black people would be better off living separately but with the same facilities.
- It should not be confused with Islam. The NOI was - and continues to be - an American movement that adopted some Islamic rules, such as observing Ramadan and refraining from drinking alcohol.
- In 1964, Malcolm X left the Nation of Islam on bad terms after an argument with its leader, Elijah Muhammad.

What happened after Malcolm X left the Nation of Islam?

The Nation of Islam firebombed his home, sent him death threats, and spoke against him publicly.

What impact did Malcolm X have on the Nation of Islam?

Malcolm X made the Nation of Islam more popular. Its membership rose from 500 in 1952 to 30,000 by 1963.

What did Malcolm X do after he left the Nation of Islam?

When Malcolm X left the Nation of Islam in 1964, he created the Organisation of African American Unity to work with other civil rights groups.

How did Malcolm X die?

Malcolm X was assassinated in New York City on 21st February, 1965, while making a speech about accepting the possibility of integration and help from white people.

Why was Malcolm X assassinated?

Malcolm X was assassinated because his views had changed following a pilgrimage to Mecca and he became more willing to work with white people to achieve integration. This angered members of the Nation of Islam.

What influence did Malcolm X have?

His influence increased after his death. There was a lot of focus on his early ideas of black pride and the use of violence in self-defence.

> **DID YOU KNOW?**
>
> **To make white people seem less intimidating, Malcolm X attempted to humiliate them.**
>
> He also attacked traditional black civil rights leaders who he believed worked too closely with white Americans.

BLACK POWER

'Our grandfathers had to run. Run, run. My generation's out of breath. We ain't running no more.' - Stokely Carmichael

What was the Black Power movement?

Influenced by Malcolm X *(p.68)*, the Black Power movement consisted of radical groups such as the Black Panther Party, which disagreed with non-violent direct action. They used the Black Power slogan and symbol to show their support.

Who first used the phrase 'black power' which led to the Black Power movement being created?

The phrase 'black power' was first used by Stokely Carmichael in 1966.

What were the aims of the Black Power movement?

Black Power activists had the following 4 primary aims:

- To reject integration with white Americans and achieve separatism, whereby they would have their own black areas or states.
- To reject the non-violent tactics and beliefs of the civil rights movement.
- To solve the social and economic challenges facing African Americans. Instead of addressing these effectively, the main civil rights movement was focused on political issues such as the right to vote.
- To increase pride in black culture and history, and promote the belief 'black is beautiful'.

Why did the Black Power movement become popular?

4 main factors contributed to the Black Power movement gaining support and popularity:

- The Civil Rights and Voting Rights Acts had not ended racism, discrimination or segregation. Change was seen as happening too slowly, increasing frustration in the black community and especially among the younger generation.
- Attention was turning away from civil rights to new issues such as the Vietnam War *(p.91)* and poverty.
- Life for those in the ghettos was getting worse, with continued discrimination when it came to education and employment. The civil rights movement, focused on ending segregation in the south, had not addressed these issues.
- It encouraged black people to be proud of their heritage.

Was the Black Power movement successful?

The Black Power movement achieved 3 main successes:

- It highlighted the importance of black culture and of taking pride in being black. Afro hairstyles and the wearing of dashikis became more common.
- In 1967, the National Committee of Negro Churchmen was created.
- The Black Panther Party implemented successful programmes such as free breakfasts for school children.

What were the limitations of the Black Power movement?

There were 3 main limitations of the Black Power movement:

- Some argue the movement alienated white people and turned some against the civil rights movement.
- It divided the civil rights movement between those that followed the traditional non-violent tactics advocated by Martin Luther King, and the more radical groups that supported the Black Power Movement's direct action.
- The government was less willing to work with the Black Power movement because it was associated with a more radical form of protest.

DID YOU KNOW?

In the 1960s, black unemployment levels remained more than double those of white unemployment.

SUPPORT FOR BLACK POWER

'To demand these God-given rights is to seek black power.' - Adam Clayton Powell Jr

What support was there for Black Power?

A number of organisations and events increased support for the Black Power movement *(p.70)*.

Why did Stokely Carmichael support the Black Power movement?

Stokely Carmichael was a prominent black civil rights activist and one of the original Freedom Riders. After being elected chairman of the SNCC *(p.56)* in 1966 he moved away from non-violent action and supported the Black Power movement *(p.70)* instead.

How did the SNCC show its support for the Black Power movement?

The SNCC *(p.56)* showed support for the Black Power movement *(p.70)* in 3 main ways:

- In 1966, Stokely Carmichael became chairman of the SNCC *(p.56)* and changed the group's direction because he was frustrated with the slow progress of non-violent tactics.
- He brought Black Power campaigners into the SNCC *(p.56)*.
- SNCC *(p.56)* became an all-black American group.

How did the Lowndes County Freedom Organisation show support for the Black Power movement?

This was an American political party founded by Stokely Carmichael in Lowndes County, Alabama, with the aim of getting black people to go out and vote. Its symbol was a black panther.

What was the March Against Fear, held in support of the Black Power movement?

This was a protest march through Mississippi led by James Meredith to highlight the violence still faced by black people. Meredith was shot and wounded on the second day, so Martin Luther King and Stokely Carmichael took his place.

What happened after the March Against Fear in support of the Black Power movement?

Support for the Black Power movement *(p.70)* was affected in 4 key ways:

- Although Martin Luther King continued to call for non-violent action, Carmichael made *militant* speeches that won over a lot of people.
- As CORE *(p.40)* and SNCC *(p.56)* became more *radical*, both organisations lost many of their original members.
- The movement terrified many white Americans and worried *moderate* African Americans.
- It did have a positive impact on many African Americans by encouraging them to take pride in their *culture* and heritage.

> **DID YOU KNOW?**
>
> A survey in Detroit found a majority of white respondents believed Black Power meant a 'violent black takeover'.

STOKELY CARMICHAEL

'If a white man wants to lynch me, that's his problem. If he's got the power to lynch me, that's my problem.' - Stokely Carmichael

Who was Stokely Carmichael?

Stokely Carmichael was chairman of the SNCC *(p.56)* and a key figure in popularising the Black Power movement *(p.70)*.

How was Stokely Carmichael involved with Black Power?

On the Meredith March, Carmichael gave his first 'black power' speech which led to the slogan spreading across America and the rise of the Black Power movement *(p.70)*.

How was Stokely Carmichael involved with Lowndes County Freedom Organisation?

In 1965, Carmichael and the SNCC *(p.56)* founded the Lowndes County Freedom Organisation. It was a political party with a black panther as its symbol, and its aim was to register African Americans to vote.

> **DID YOU KNOW?**
>
> Carmichael changed his name to Kwame Ture and moved from the United States to Guinea, Africa, becoming an aide to the Guinean president.

MEXICO OLYMPICS, 1968

'How can you ask someone to live in the world and not have something to say about injustice?' - John Carlos

What happened at the 1968 Mexico Olympics?

At the 1968 Mexico Olympics, American athletes Tommie Smith and John Carlos gave the Black Power salute as they received their gold and bronze medals for the men's 200m race.

What happened after the 1968 Mexico Olympics?

There were 2 main results of their actions:

- There was booing from the crowds and both men were suspended from the US Olympic squad.
- As well as being criticised by the media and politicians, they each received death threats. However, many young black people were inspired to join the Black Power movement *(p.70)* as a result of their actions.

> **DID YOU KNOW?**
>
> **Tommie Smith and John Carlos received death threats when they returned home to America but were eventually able to return to sport.**
>
> The Australian who shared the podium with them after gaining the silver medal, Peter Norman, was excluded from sports on is return home for standing with them.

BLACK PANTHERS, 1966

'I have no doubt that the revolution will triumph.' - Huey Newton, 1973

What were the Black Panthers?

The Black Panthers was a political group that represented militant black power views. Its full name was the Black Panther Party for Self Defense. Members were known for wearing all black clothing, including a beret and leather jacket.

Who started the Black Panthers?

The Black Panthers were founded by Huey Newton and Bobby Searle.

When were the Black Panthers founded?

The organisation was started in October 1966.

Where were the Black Panthers founded?

The Black Panthers began in Oakland, California.

What did the Black Panthers believe in?

The Black Panthers held 3 main beliefs:

- White police and officials would not support or work for the interests of black people.
- Black communities should have black officials.
- They could work with white people who supported their aims.

What was the Black Panthers' 10-point programme?

The Black Panthers had a 10-point programme they believed would improve their communities. It included:

- Full employment for African Americans.
- Better housing.
- Better education.

- ☑ An end to police brutality.

What did the Black Panthers do as well as the 10-point programme?
The Black Panthers were involved in 4 other main activities:
- ☑ Organising safety patrols of their communities.
- ☑ Running courses on black history.
- ☑ Organising free healthcare.
- ☑ Running breakfast clubs for poor black children.

Were the Black Panthers violent?
There were 3 main issues the Black Panthers were linked with violence:
- ☑ Members carried guns and there were frequent shootouts in the ghettos.
- ☑ They often clashed with the police and some of their funding came from criminal activities.
- ☑ Leader Huey Newton was charged with murder in 1968.

How did people react to the Black Panthers?
People reacted to the Black Panthers in 2 main ways:
- ☑ The white community reacted with fear because they saw the group as violent and radical. As many members carried guns, which was allowed in California as long as they were visible, people saw them as dangerous.
- ☑ They were under surveillance by the FBI and other law enforcement agencies.

Did the Black Panthers have many members?
Although there were Black Panther groups in 25 cities by 1968, overall the organisation never had more than around 2,000 members.

DID YOU KNOW?

The Panther newsletter had a circulation of a quarter of a million by 1969.

RACE RIOTS, 1964-67

'We were so scared!' - a witness to the Harlem riots

What were the riots of 1964 to 1967?
There were 329 major race riots in cities across America between 1964 and 1967, caused by the problems black people faced in the ghettos.

Where did the riots of 1964 to 1967 take place?
The race riots of 1965 to 1967 took place in 8 main locations:
- ☑ Los Angeles in 1965.
- ☑ New York in 1964.
- ☑ Chicago and Cleveland in 1966.
- ☑ Newark and Detroit in 1967.

- Washington and Cleveland in 1968.

What were the causes of the riots between 1964 to 1967?

There were 6 main causes of the race riots:

- Schools were often run down, poorly funded and badly equipped.
- Housing and living conditions were poor.
- There was police discrimination against black people, wrongful and violent arrests, and police brutality towards African Americans.
- Black people mostly had low-paid, unskilled jobs. Unemployment figures were double those of white people.
- Authorities did little to help with problems in the ghettos. Complaints from black neighbourhoods were ignored.
- The assassination of Martin Luther King *(p.78)* in April 1968 was a key trigger.

What happened during the riots of 1964 to 1967?

Over 200 people were killed, thousands were injured and 27,000 were arrested. There was also at least $45 million worth of damage caused.

What happened in Los Angeles during the riots of 1964 to 1967?

There were main 4 events during the Los Angeles race riots:

- They happened in the Watts district.
- They happened between 11th and 17th August, 1965.
- More than 14,000 National Guardsmen were called in to deal with the riots.
- There were over 4,000 arrests, 34 deaths and massive property damage.

What was the result of the riots of 1964 to 1967?

The riots had 5 important consequences:

- The riots drew attention to the severity of the problems that existed in the ghettos.
- The government ordered an investigation into the causes of the riots, which led to the Kerner Report *(p.76)*.
- President Johnson *(p.82)* began to allocate more money for improvements and ordered an investigation into the reasons for the riots.
- Before his assassination, Martin Luther King began to campaign in the north.
- The riots shocked America and the civil rights movement lost support because of the violence.

DID YOU KNOW?

Riots broke out in some 125 cities.

KERNER REPORT, 1968

'Our nation is moving towards two societies, one black, one white - separate and unequal.' - Kerner Report

What was the Kerner Report?
The Kerner Report was a government report outlining the reasons for the race riots that had broken out in several American cities between 1965 and 1967.

When was the Kerner Report published?
The Kerner Report was issued in February 1968.

Who ordered the Kerner Report to be published?
President Johnson *(p.82)* ordered the Kerner Report to be written.

What were the main findings of the Kerner report?
There were 5 main findings:
- The main issue the report found was the racism was a significant long-term problem in America.
- Police brutality towards African Americans was a significant problem.
- As many as 40% of African Americans lived in poverty and this created very poor conditions in the ghettos. Poverty was caused by discrimination and segregation.
- The way the authorities responded to problems needed to change.
- The extent and level of violence during the riots had been exaggerated by the media, which had further inflamed the situation.

> **DID YOU KNOW?**
>
> **The Kerner Report identified poverty as one of the key causes of the race riots.**
>
> In 2018, 22% of black Americans lived in poverty compared to just 9% of whites. In 2020, inequality continues to be a serious issue with black American unemployment levels twice of those among white people.

CAMPAIGN IN THE NORTH, 1968

'I have seen many demonstrations in the south but I have never seen anything so hostile and so hateful as I've seen here today.' - Martin Luther King in Chicago, 1966

What was Martin Luther King's campaign in the north?
Martin Luther King and the SCLC *(p.41)* began a non-violent direct action campaign in Chicago focused on several issues. It was called the Chicago Freedom Movement, or Chicago Campaign.

When was Martin Luther King's campaign in the north?
The campaign in the north, or the Chicago Freedom Movement, started on 7th January, 1966, and ended in 1967.

What were the aims of Martin Luther King's campaign in the north?

The campaign focused on three issues - education, housing and employment.

What operation was established during Martin Luther King's campaign in the north?

Operation Breadbasket was established to organise boycotts of businesses and put pressure on them to employ more black workers.

What action was taken during Martin Luther King's campaign in the north?

Along with other leaders, Martin Luther King met with the authorities in a bid to improve housing conditions.

What were the main obstacles encountered by Martin Luther King's campaign in the north?

There were 4 main issues with the campaign:

- Many black politicians were among those who opposed it.
- There was a lack of connection between the SCLC *(p.41)* and the ghetto gangs.
- Riots started before Martin Luther King's *(p.52)* planned march through white neighbourhoods had even begun. He appealed for calm but was ignored.
- The campaign did not receive as much good publicity as anticipated.

What were the results of Martin Luther King's campaign in the north?

The campaign had 2 main results:

- The march went ahead as planned and a violent white backlash followed.
- The Mayor of Chicago was keen for the protests to end, so came to an agreement on fair housing rates. He also pledged more public housing would be built.

What was successful about Martin Luther King's campaign in the north?

More black people were employed by white-owned and run companies.

What were the failures of the Martin Luther King's campaign in the North?

The campaign failed in 2 key areas:

- Martin Luther King was unable to prevent violence on both sides.
- The Mayor of Chicago failed to honour the agreement he had made and housing costs and shortages remained the same.

DID YOU KNOW?

Some historians argue that the differences in thinking between Malcolm X and Martin Luther King in their later years were exaggerated, and both actually shared many common beliefs.

MARTIN LUTHER KING ASSASSINATION, 1968

'When he died, I think something died in all of us. Something died in America.' - John Lewis, one of the original Freedom Riders

What were the details of Martin Luther King's assassination?
Martin Luther King was shot at a motel in Memphis, Tennessee. He was rushed to hospital but died within an hour.

Where was Martin Luther King's assassination?
The assassination took place on a balcony at the Lorraine Motel.

When was the assassination of Martin Luther King?
Martin Luther King was assassinated at 6.01pm CST on 4th April, 1968.

Who carried out Martin Luther King's assassination?
Martin Luther King was murdered by a white supremacist called James Earl Ray.

Why was Martin Luther King in Memphis at the time of his assassination?
There were 2 main reasons for Martin Luther King's *(p.52)* presence in Memphis:
- ☑ He was preparing to march in support of refuse collectors who were striking for better pay and working conditions.
- ☑ He had also planned a Poor People's Campaign *(p.79)*.

What were the consequences the of the assassination of Martin Luther King?
The death of Martin Luther King had 3 important consequences:
- ☑ There were riots in 172 cities after his assassination.
- ☑ The Poor People's Campaign *(p.79)*, which King had been planning up to his death, struggled without his leadership.
- ☑ The 1968 Civil Rights Act was passed into law.

Why did the civil rights movement lose support after Martin Luther King's assassination?
There were two primary reasons the civil rights movement lost support following Martin Luther King's assassination:
- ☑ Once King was gone, many white people felt there was nobody left in the civil rights movement they could relate to. Without that connection, they began to oppose the more radical demands that were made.
- ☑ The previously non-violent SNCC *(p.56)* changed its stance to 'national'.

DID YOU KNOW?

Martin Luther King's tomb is located at The Martin Luther King Jr Center for Nonviolent and Social Change in Atlanta, Georgia.
The centre is the official memorial to his work.

CIVIL RIGHTS ACT, 1968

'We have come some of the way, not near all of it. There is much yet to do.' - President Lyndon B Johnson, 1968

What was the 1968 Civil Rights Act?

The 1968 Act provided increased protection for civil rights activists and harsher penalties for rioters. Housing policies were also made more equal.

Which president passed the Civil Rights Act 1968?

The 1968 Act was signed into law by President Lyndon B Johnson *(p.82)*.

> **DID YOU KNOW?**
>
> The Civil Rights Act of 1968 is also called the Fair Housing Act.
> Its aim was to make discrimination on the basis of race, religion or national origin illegal when it came to housing.

POOR PEOPLE'S CAMPAIGN, 1968

'Tell Dr King to bring the people to Washington.' - Senator Robert Kennedy

What was the Poor People's Campaign?

The Poor People's Campaign was a march on Washington *(p.61)* to highlight the economic injustice experienced by poor people in America.

Who organized the Poor People's Campaign?

Martin Luther King and the SCLC *(p.41)* organised the Poor People's Campaign.

When did the Poor People's Campaign take place?

The Poor People's Campaign was set up in December 1967 and took place between 12th May and 24th June, 1968.

What happened during the Poor People's Campaign?

There were 4 main events during the Poor People's Campaign:

- ☑ Protesters arrived in Washington on 12th May, 1968.
- ☑ They built 'Resurrection City' - a camp made of tents and temporary buildings - on the Mall.
- ☑ The weather was terrible.
- ☑ The camp was closed by the National Guard.

What were the results of the Poor People's Campaign?

There were 3 main results of the Poor People's Campaign:

- ☑ Following Martin Luther King's assassination *(p.78)* the groups involved could not agree on what tactics to use.
- ☑ Many supporters left Washington before the march began.
- ☑ Poor organisation meant it failed and damaged the image of the civil rights movement.

> **DID YOU KNOW?**
>
> King's inspiration for the Poor People's Campaign came when he wept upon seeing hungry children share an apple and crackers for lunch.

JOHN F KENNEDY

'... a great and good man.' President Lyndon B Johnson, 1963

Who was President Kennedy?

John F Kennedy, commonly referred to as JFK, was the 35th President of the United States.

When was Kennedy president?

John F Kennedy was president between January 1961 and November 1963.

What was Kennedy's background?

Kennedy's background included the following:

- He came from an Irish-American family which was very wealthy and heavily involved in politics.
- He went to Harvard University and studied politics. He wrote his dissertation on Britain's policy of the appeasement of Adolf Hitler.
- He was in the US navy and served in the Second World War, where he was seriously injured when his boat was destroyed by the Japanese.

What were the key events of Kennedy's presidency?

The key events of Kennedy's presidency included the following:

- Kennedy created the Peace Corps in 1961.
- The Bay of Pigs Invasion in Cuba, in April 1961.
- In May 1961 he pledged America would put a man on the moon by the end of the decade.
- The Berlin Wall was built in 1961.
- The Cuban Missile Crisis took place in October 1962.
- He signed the Limited Nuclear Test Ban Treaty in August 1963.

What were Kennedy's beliefs about the Cold War?

Kennedy was anti-communist and, like his predecessors, was committed to containing communism. However, he was aware of the dangers of nuclear warfare after tensions were brought to the brink during the Cuban Missile Crisis, and wanted to reduce the chances of nuclear war.

What was President Kennedy's role in the Bay of Pigs invasion?

Kennedy attempted to implement a counter-revolution in Cuba by sending in Cuban exiles. The aim was to make it look like the USA wasn't involved. However, the plan failed.

What was President Kennedy's involvement with the Cuban Missile Crisis?
In 1962, two U2 spy planes spotted what looked like missiles in Cuba. This led to a tense 13 days where Kennedy deliberated what to do. He decided to set up a naval blockade and managed to prevent nuclear war.

What was President Kennedy's role in Vietnam?
President Kennedy continued to support South Vietnam with money, military advisers and commandos.

How did President Kennedy die?
Kennedy was assassinated in November 1963 in Dallas, Texas.

Why was President Kennedy in Dallas?
Kennedy was in Dallas because he needed to win support from the southern Democrats, nicknamed the Dixiecrats *(p.54)*, for his Civil Rights bill.

DID YOU KNOW?

The Kennedy family was rich and powerful.
JFK's brothers, Robert and Ted, both became famous senators.

JOHN F KENNEDY AND CIVIL RIGHTS

'It ought to to be possible, in short, for every American to enjoy the privileges of being American without regard to his race or his colour.' - President Kennedy, 1963

What policies did John F Kennedy introduce?
John F Kennedy *(p.80)* introduced a range of new policies in his 'New Frontier'. These included education, the economy, and civil rights.

What policies did John F Kennedy introduce for the economy?
Kennedy *(p.80)* had 2 main economic policies:
- He cut taxes to give people more money to spend.
- He made $900 million available to businesses to create new jobs, and gave grants to companies so they could buy new hi-tech equipment and train their workers to use it.

What policies did John F Kennedy introduce on poverty?
Kennedy's *(p.80)* social policies on poverty included:
- Making $4.9 billion available for loans to improve housing, clear slums and build roads.
- His Social Security Act, which improved benefits for the elderly and unemployed.

What policies did John F Kennedy introduce on education?
Kennedy's *(p.80)* education policies included:
- He established the Peace Corps, an organisation sending volunteers overseas to help people in developing countries. They worked as teachers, doctors, nurses and technical advisers.

- JFK *(p.80)* was also keen to introduce an education law to give more money to schools.

What policies did John F Kennedy introduce on civil rights?

Kennedy *(p.80)* took 5 main actions in support of civil rights:

- He gave more important jobs to African Americans than any other president had done previously, such as appointing lawyer Thurgood Marshall to the courts.
- He wanted to see civil rights laws introduced, but was assassinated before they were passed.
- He created the CEEO - Commission on Equal Employment Opportunity - to ensure all people working for the federal government had equal employment opportunities.
- He issued executive orders that federal troops should be deployed to the University of Mississippi to support and protect James Meredith.
- He also applied personal pressure to get escorts for the Freedom Riders, to ensure their safety.

> **DID YOU KNOW?**
>
> Despite his health problems, Kennedy served in the US Navy during the Second World War.

LYNDON B JOHNSON

'The challenge of the next half-century is whether we have the wisdom to use that wealth to enrich and elevate our national life.' - President Lyndon B Johnson, 1964

Who was President Johnson?

Lyndon B Johnson was the 36th President of the United States.

When was Johnson president?

Lyndon B Johnson was in office from 1963 to 1969.

What was Johnson's background?

Johnson's background included the following:

- He did not come from a wealthy background, and this shaped the kind of president he wanted to be.
- His ambitions as president included creating a 'Great Society' that was fair to everyone.
- Despite his ambitions he is most remembered for his role in the Vietnam War *(p.91)*.

What were the key events in Johnson's presidency?

Some of the key events of Johnson's presidency included the following:

- He took over as president after the assassination of John F Kennedy *(p.80)*.
- He signed the Civil Rights Act of 1964, which made discrimination based on race or colour, sex, religion or national origin illegal.
- Congress passed the Gulf of Tonkin Resolution, giving Johnson the power to pursue military action in Vietnam in August 1964.
- Martin Luther King Junior *(p.52)* was assassinated in April 1968.
- The Tet Offensive happened in June 1968.

What were Johnson's views on the Cold War?

Johnson was anti-communist and, like Truman, Eisenhower and Kennedy *(p.80)*, he was committed to stopping the spread of communism.

What was President Johnson's role in Vietnam?

President Johnson escalated the USA's role in the war in 1965 by ordering the bombing of North Vietnam (Operation Rolling Thunder), and sending in the first US combat troops there. He also diverted funds from the welfare program to pay for the war.

How did President Lyndon B Johnson support the civil rights movement?

President Johnson supported the civil rights movement in 4 main ways:

- He continued the work of President Kennedy *(p.80)* and appointed African Americans into several high profile positions.
- He also signed the Civil Rights 1964 and Voting Rights 1965 acts into law.
- He issued executive orders that meant state troops could be federalised and used to escort the Selma marchers to safety.
- He had a good relationship with the Dixiecrats *(p.54)*, and he used this to apply personal pressure on southern politicians to get them to support the Civil Rights bill.

> **DID YOU KNOW?**
>
> **Johnson was sworn in as president on Airforce One following Kennedy's assassination.**
>
> A female federal judge, Sarah T Hughes, conducted the swearing in. Also present was JFK's widow, Jacqueline Kennedy, wearing a jacket stained with her husband's blood.

RICHARD NIXON

'Unless we in America work to preserve freedom, there will be no freedom.' - President Richard Nixon, 1973

Did President Nixon support civil rights for black people?

President Nixon was not as committed to the civil rights of African Americans as President Johnson *(p.82)*.

What changes did Nixon make to support civil rights?

He took 4 key actions that helped African Americans.

- He encouraged African Americans people to start their own businesses and to buy their own homes.
- He continued the policy of affirmative action started by President Johnson *(p.82)*, which involved encouraging employers to deliberately choose an African American person over a white one.
- More African American officials were appointed to roles in his government.
- In 1972, the terms of the Voting Rights Act *(p.67)* of 1965 were amended to completely ban literacy tests.

How successful were Nixon's actions for civil rights?

Civil rights had progressed a lot since 1954. However, African Americans were still paid less than their white counterparts, continued to live in ghettos, and were still poorly treated by the police.

> **DID YOU KNOW?**
>
> **President Richard Nixon hosted the largest ever dinner at the White House.**
> It was held to welcome American prisoners of war home from Vietnam.

OTHER PROTEST MOVEMENTS

'It is better to protest than to accept injustice.' - Rosa Parks

What other protest movements were there in the 1960s?

During the 1960s, people did not only protest for civil rights. Other movements began to try and change society.

What other protest groups were there in the 1960s?

There were 3 main other protest groups:

- Students, who protested about a range of issues from civil rights to their education.
- Women, over equal rights.
- People who were opposed to the Vietnam War *(p.91)*.

What caused people to protest in the 1960s?

There were 6 main reasons people protested in the 1960s:

- Young people who took part in the civil rights movement, both black and white, used their experience to highlight other aspects of society with which they were unhappy.
- Women also felt encouraged to campaign for their rights. Many were angry at the lack of change and the unfairness they experienced in post-1945 America.
- Many people expected life to change when the Second World War ended and were disillusioned and unhappy when it did not.
- During the 1950s, many teenagers began to rebel against their parents. By the 1960s, a new counter-culture began to develop in which young people questioned their parents' society.
- During the 1960s there was a huge rise in the numbers of homes with televisions. Coverage of protests attracted more people to join them and helped raise awareness of racism and inequality.
- America's role in the Vietnam War *(p.91)* became a focal point of the new protest movement as it impacted the lives of students and women, and went against all the counter-culture stood for.

What other reasons were there for student protest in the 1960s?

There were 3 other main reasons students protested in the 1960s:

- The increase in the birth rate after the Second World War meant there were a lot of young people who wanted their views to be heard.
- Musicians like Jimi Hendrix and Bob Dylan communicated ideas which encouraged young people to challenge their parents' society.

- Other developments, such as labour-saving devices and the contraceptive pill, caused women to question their roles in society.

> **DID YOU KNOW?**
>
> Between 15,000 and 25,000 people attended the March on Washington to End the War in Vietnam on April 17th, 1965.
>
> The march was organised by the Students for a Democratic Society.

STUDENT PROTEST

'Students voted for human dignity.' - poster slogan at a student protest

What were students protesting about in the 1960s?

During the 1960s and 1970s, students campaigned on a variety of issues affecting society including women's rights, poverty and the Vietnam War *(p.91)*.

When were the students protests in the 1960s?

The main student protests started in 1964 and continued until 1970.

What caused students to protest in the 1960s?

There were 5 main reasons for the student protests:

- There was a big rise in the number of people going to college after the Second World War, and many students became increasingly concerned with American social issues.
- Students wanted more of a say in their education.
- The civil rights movement influenced the students and taught them how to protest.
- They were impacted by the Vietnam War *(p.91)* as the average age of soldiers in the conflict was 19 - their own age group.
- The development of a counter-culture, such as the hippy movement, and the development of drugs like the pill and LSD influenced students to protest against the established culture of their parents' generation.

How did students protest during the 1960s?

Students protested in 6 main ways:

- Some joined existing groups such as SNCC *(p.56)* or CORE *(p.40)*.
- Some joined the Students for a Democratic Society, or SDS.
- Many joined anti-Vietnam War *(p.91)* protests.
- Some became hippies.
- Many followed the non-violent protest example of the early civil rights movement and took part in sit-ins and marches.
- Some students became more radical and used extreme methods, such as the Weatherman or Weather Underground - a small, violent offshoot of Students for a Democratic Society.

What were the main events of the student protests during the 1960s?

There were 3 main student protests:

- ✅ The sit-ins and marches at Berkeley *(p.88)* University in 1964, which created the Berkeley Free Speech Movement.
- ✅ The protests at Columbia University in 1968 which involved the occupation of university buildings by students.
- ✅ The Kent State *(p.89)* University protests in 1970 which resulted in 4 students being shot dead by the National Guard.

What did the student protests achieve?

The student movement *(p.86)* did have some successes but it was limited for 3 main reasons:

- ✅ The student movement *(p.86)* never gained the general support of American society, unlike the civil rights movement.
- ✅ While some university groups like the Berkeley *(p.88)* Free Speech Movement did achieve their aims, the main problem for the student movement *(p.86)* was the large number of issues it protested about.
- ✅ Opposition to the Vietnam War *(p.91)* was the only issue the student movement *(p.86)* was united on.

DID YOU KNOW?

In 1968, students at San Francisco State University went on strike for five months!

STUDENT MOVEMENT

'We have a saying in the movement that we don't trust anybody over 30.' - Jack Weinberg

What was the student movement?

The student movement was a left-wing crusade which wanted to transform American society. It focused on perceived social, political and economic injustices of the time.

When did the student movement develop?

The student movement began to gain momentum at the end of the 1960s and in the early 1970s.

Why did the student movement develop?

There were 4 key reasons the student movement developed:

- ✅ Students wanted a greater say in their education at college and university.
- ✅ Students wanted a form of participatory democracy in which people had more say in politics and more control over decisions made by the government.
- ✅ Students wanted to end racism and fight for civil rights.
- ✅ Students were against the Vietnam War *(p.91)*.

Why did the student movement oppose the Vietnam War?

The student movement against the Vietnam War *(p.91)* grew for 8 key reasons:

- ✅ Media coverage turned people against the war.
- ✅ 12 per cent of soldiers that fought in the war ended up either dead or seriously injured. The number of amputations was approximately 300 per cent higher than in the Second World War.
- ✅ The average age of an American GI killed in Vietnam was 23.
- ✅ 2,000,000 men were forced to fight in Vietnam between 1964 and 1972 as a result of the draft.
- ✅ Leading figures like Martin Luther King and Muhammad Ali highlighted issues of racial inequality in the US forces.

- People did not like the corruption and brutality of the South Vietnamese government as it was undemocratic.
- Even politicians began to question the war, which was distracting the government from pressing domestic issues like education and healthcare.
- The USA was losing against the Vietcong. Events like the Tet Offensive and My Lai Massacre brought this home to the American people.

How did students and hippies protest against the war in Vietnam as part of the student movement?

Examples of protests and demonstrations included:

- 500,000 people came together in Washington on 15th November, 1969, to listen to speeches and songs about ending the war. It was the biggest anti-war protest in US history.
- Hippies protested by rejecting the traditional American way of life. Not working or going to school, growing hair long and taking illegal drugs was seen as a rejection of government and authority.
- Student protests became increasingly violent and there were many clashes with police.
- In August 1970, at the University of Wisconsin-Madison in Wisconsin, a bomb was detonated by student protesters. One person was killed and several others injured.
- In May 1970, there were protests at the Kent State *(p.89)* University which resulted in the deaths of 4 students.

Why did the student movement gain media coverage?

The protestors were a small minority of the 8.5 million students in the US, but they attracted a lot of media interest because most of them were white, middle-class, and outwardly rejecting the values of their parents' generation.

What did the Students for a Democratic Society do in the student movement?

There are 5 key facts to note about the Students for a Democratic Society:

- It was a student activist organisation, led by Tom Hayden, that grew to 3,000 members on 80 campuses by 1965. By the end of the decade it had over 100,000 members in 150 colleges.
- It held its first meeting in 1960. It released a statement called 'Port Huron', which set out its aims to campaign against racism and war, and in support of human rights.
- It participated in civil rights protests and campaigned for better students' rights in universities and colleges. It also protested against university rules.
- It grew considerably because students greatly opposed American involvement in the Vietnam War *(p.91)*.
- It split into different groups by 1969 due to internal disagreements.

What was the Weatherman student movement?

There are 4 key facts to note about the Weatherman movement:

- It was a radical student group created in 1969 when the Students for a Democratic Society collapsed.
- It was willing to incite and use violence to stop the Vietnam War *(p.91)* and create a revolution.
- It was responsible for several acts of domestic terrorism, including bomb attacks between 1970 and 1971 in New York, Boston and Washington.
- The members of the group were hunted by the FBI.

What was the significance of the student movement to the Vietnam War?

The student movement was significant as it was a key factor in the eventual withdrawal of US forces from Vietnam.

> **DID YOU KNOW?**
>
> **'Hell no, we won't go.' - popular student slogan against the Vietnam War.**
> Over 30,000 people left the United States to avoid the draft.

BERKELEY FREE SPEECH MOVEMENT, 1964-65

'There's a time when the operation of the machine becomes so odious, makes you so sick at heart, that you can't take part.' - Mario Savio, 1964

What was the Berkeley Free Speech Movement?
The Berkeley Free Speech Movement was formed by a group of students who challenged Berkeley University's regulations on free speech.

When did the Berkeley Free Speech Movement begin?
The Berkeley Free Speech Movement started in September 1964 and lasted for the academic year, ending in 1965.

Why did students at Berkeley protest?
In September 1964, students were banned from protesting on university grounds. The protests demanded the university reversed this ban and allowed freedom of speech.

What were the events at Berkeley?
There were 4 main events during the protests:

- Students ignored the ban and continued protesting. Some were suspended, and the remaining students congregated in the university's administration building demanding to be suspended too.
- The police were called and one student was arrested. The remaining students blocked the police from leaving for 32 hours. Eventually the students agreed to leave.
- After this, students created the Free Speech Movement to protest against the university preventing them from holding protests on campus. They produced thousands of leaflets and held many meetings.
- In November 1964, those students who had been suspended were charged with breaking university rules. The Free Speech Movement organised a sit-in in a university building, supported by 6,000 students. It took the police 12 hours to make 750 arrests.

What was the impact of the Berkeley Free Speech Movement?
University staff voted to allow protesting on campus but there were strict rules about how, when and where protests could be carried out.

> **DID YOU KNOW?**
>
> **Lawyers defended over 800 students who were arrested in December 1964.**
> At the time it was the largest mass arrest in California's history.

KENT STATE UNIVERSITY PROTESTS, 1970

'This summer I hear the drumming. Four dead in Ohio.' - lyrics from 'Ohio', by Neil Young

What was the Kent State Protest?

The Kent State Protest, or Kent State shootings, involved the shooting and killing of unarmed university students who were protesting against the Vietnam War *(p.91)*.

When did the Kent State University protest shootings happen?

The Kent State protest occurred between 1st and 4th May, 1970. The shootings took place on the final day.

Where did the Kent State Shootings happen?

The shootings happened at Kent State University in the state of Ohio.

Why did the Kent State University protest shootings happen?

There were 2 main reasons for the shootings:

- Protestors were demonstrating at the university against the Vietnam War *(p.91)*. This was prompted by Nixon's announcement of the invasion of Cambodia and the need for 150,000 more US troops.
- The Ohio state governor had sent in the National Guard to stop the demonstrations that had taken place all weekend. On the Monday, the protests turned violent and events escalated to the shootings.

What were the key events in the Kent State University protest shootings?

There were 6 key events in the Kent State University protest shootings:

- President Nixon announced to the American public that US forces had invaded Cambodia on 30th April, 1970.
- Protests across America took place the next day at many colleges and universities, including Kent State University.
- Protests continued over the weekend, often escalating to clashes between protesters and police. Windows were smashed and police cars vandalised.
- With further protests planned for Monday, 4th May, amid fears of continued violence, 1,000 National Guardsmen were sent to stop them.
- Just after midday, violence erupted. Students threw rocks and the National Guardsmen responded with tear gas.
- In the chaos, at 12.24pm, some of the National Guardsmen started shooting at the protesters. 4 students, including one called Jeffrey Miller, were killed and a further 9 were injured.

How did the Kent State Protest begin?

The Kent State shootings started when National Guardsmen fired their guns into a crowd of student protesters and students. The reasons for the shooting remain unclear.

How did the Kent State Protest develop?

There were 5 main developments over the first four days of May:

- There were clashes between anti-war protesters and pro-war supporters.
- There were student demonstrations over the following days. These included sit-ins and the students occupying some university buildings, as well as setting fire to the Reserve Officers' Training Office on campus.
- The state governor sent in 900 National Guardsmen with tear gas and rifles.
- The students threw gas canisters and bricks at the National Guard.
- The National Guard fired into the crowd and killed four students. Nine other people were injured.

What happened to the National Guardsmen that had carried out the shootings at the Kent State University protest?

The government investigated the shootings and a report stated that the guardsmen's actions were "unnecessary, unwarranted, and inexcusable". 8 of them were arrested but there was not enough evidence to prosecute.

What was the public reaction to the shootings at the Kent State Protest?

There were 3 main reactions to the shooting:

- The public was horrified by the shootings, which caused outrage across America.
- However, there was some support for the National Guardsmen who had shot at the students.
- There were protests at other universities, and about 2 million students went on strike because of the killings.

Why were the shootings at the Kent State Protest controversial?

The students killed in the Kent State shootings were white and middle class, which was why there was such public outrage. When two black students were shot and 12 injured during an anti-war protest at Jackson State University, there was very little publicity or reaction.

What was significant about the shootings at the Kent State University protest?

The shootings were significant as it strengthened the anti-war movement further and led to increased calls for America to withdraw from Vietnam.

DID YOU KNOW?

Neil Young wrote 'Ohio' in response to the shootings.
It was sung by Crosby, Stills, Nash and Young.

HIPPY MOVEMENT

'Make love, not war.' - popular anti-war slogan

Who were the hippies?

Hippies were young people who rejected society, choosing not to work or go to college.

Why did the hippy movement develop?

There were 2 main reasons the hippy movement developed:

- A counter-culture developed in the 1960s which was against the culture of older generations and the 'establishment' - those in authority such as the government and police.
- It was a reaction to the political and social issues of the time. For example, the hippies objected to the actions of the US government *(p. 16)* in the Vietnam War *(p. 91)*.

What was the hippy movement?

There were 3 main activities the hippies were involved in:

- They promoted messages of peace, love and happiness and experimented with sex, drugs and art, especially music.

- They lived in communes or travelled around in buses or vans. They usually wore their hair long and unstyled, and colourful clothing.
- They were involved in various protest movements and campaigned on environmental issues.

Was the hippy movement a success?

The hippy movement had 2 main effects:

- Many Americans viewed hippies as 'wasters' who corrupted society. With the exception of the civil rights movement, hippies had little impact on government policies.
- While few young Americans actually became hippies they did adopt some aspects of the movement, such as listening to rock music and experimenting with drugs.

> **DID YOU KNOW?**
> To demonstrate their pacifism, hippies would put flowers in the barrels of soldiers' guns during protests.

VIETNAM WAR

'We do this to increase the confidence of the brave people of South Vietnam who have bravely born this brutal battle.' President Lyndon B Johnson, 1965

What was the Vietnam War?

The Vietnam War was a lengthy conflict which began in 1954, after Vietnam was divided into two. North Vietnam wanted to reunite the country under communism while South Vietnam, assisted by the USA, fought to keep this from happening.

When did the Vietnam War happen?

Officially the Vietnam War began in 1955 and ended in 1975. However, some events prior to 1955 are important in order to understand how the war developed.

What were the key phases in the Vietnam War?

There were 4 key phases to the Vietnam War, including:

- The 1st phase of the conflict was between 1945 and 1954. The Vietminh fought to drive French imperial rule from Vietnam. This ended with the signing of the Geneva Accords and Vietnam being split into 2 countries. This period is called the First Indochina War.
- The 2nd phase, between 1957 and 1963, saw the leader of South Vietnam, Ngo Dinh Diem, fight a bitter civil war against the Vietcong which was supported by Ho Chi Minh's government in the north. This ended with Diem being assassinated just weeks before the American president, John F Kennedy, was assassinated in November 1963.
- The 3rd phase, from 1964 to 1968, saw a huge escalation in the conflict between America - which before 1964 had no direct military presence in the region - and North Vietnam. America was fighting the Vietcong directly in order to stop a communist takeover in the south.
- The 4th phase of the conflict, between 1969 and 1973, was defined by America's desire to withdraw from Vietnam and its actions to bring US troops home. The last military personnel were withdrawn from the region in 1973.

Who was involved in the Vietnam War?

There were a number of different parties and nations involved in the war including:

- France - the roots of the conflict begin with its attempts to maintain rule in Vietnam after the Second World War.
- Ho Chi Minh's Vietminh, which fought to remove all foreign influences from Vietnam. After the division of the country in 1954, under the Geneva Accords, Ho Chi Minh would become the leader of North Vietnam. Much of the war featured his battles with the Americans as he tried to take over South Vietnam and unite the two nations.
- The USA was involved in the conflict from July 1950, when it tried to assist the French against the Vietminh.
- Both China and the USSR were involved, supporting Ho Chi Minh from the start of conflict as he tried to drive out the French.
- South Vietnam was a new country created in 1954 under the Geneva Accords, and America's presence there was a bid to stop a communist takeover.
- Cambodia and Laos were drawn into the conflict on occasions, due to shared borders with Vietnam.

Why did the USA get involved in the Vietnam War?

The USA was concerned about the Domino Theory and could not allow South Vietnam to become communist. It became increasingly involved in supporting South Vietnam as part of its containment policy.

How did the USA get involved in the Vietnam War?

There were 3 key stages to American involvement in the Vietnam War:

- From 1950, the USA gave $1.6 billion dollars in aid to South Vietnam, and sent political advisers.
- From 1960, it began to send military advisers to train the South Vietnamese Army.
- From 1965, it sent American combat troops to Vietnam and became fully involved in the war.

Which US presidents got involved in the Vietnam War?

The USA's involvement in Vietnam spanned 5 different presidents:

- President Truman, who started sending military aid to the French to fight the Vietminh.
- President Eisenhower, who was the first to send military aid to the new South Vietnamese government in January 1955.
- President Kennedy *(p.80)*, who began increasing the number of US military advisors sent to Vietnam to train the ARVN - the South Vietnamese army.
- President Johnson *(p.82)*, who committed the first US boots on the ground to Vietnam in March 1965.
- President Nixon, who led the withdrawal of all American troops from Vietnam.

Why did people protest against the Vietnam War?

One of the defining features of the Vietnam War was the anti-war movement that developed in the USA. Protesters objected to many aspects, including the cost, the rising number of deaths, atrocities committed by US soldiers, and the draft system.

How did people protest against the Vietnam War?

Protests included mass rallies, sit-ins, and the burning of draft cards.

What was the cost of the Vietnam War?

The Vietnam War cost much more than anticipated - a total of $167 billion.

What was Congress's response to the Vietnam War after the invasion of Cambodia?

Congress responded to the Vietnam War in 4 important ways after the invasion of Cambodia in 1970.

- The Gulf of Tonkin Resolution was revoked.
- Military funding was limited.
- A cut-off date of 30th June 1970 was set for troops to leave Cambodia.

- A deadline of December 1971 was set for the total withdrawal of US troops from Vietnam.

What were the reasons for the Vietnam War being unwinnable?

Many historians argue the Vietnam War was unwinnable for 9 key reasons:

- North Vietnam was determined to withstand the USA.
- The US military struggled to defeat the Vietcong's guerrilla tactics.
- The war had to stay within limits if the USA was to avoid confrontation with China or the USSR.
- The Americans knew little about the country.
- Vietnamese peasants were alienated by American policy, and the tactics used by the US military.
- Vietnam had a history of opposing conquering countries, such as France and Japan.
- The USA was unable to close the Ho Chi Minh Trail, which was used to supply the Vietcong.
- American soldiers were unused to jungle warfare, while the Vietnamese were experts.
- The South Vietnamese government had been unstable ever since the death of Diem in 1963.

DID YOU KNOW?

Australia, New Zealand and South Korea also fought in Vietnam.

OPPOSITION TO VIETNAM WAR

'You send the best of this country off to be shot and maimed.' - Eartha Kitt, American singer

What media coverage was there of the Vietnam War?

US media coverage continued to expand as the war continued. In 1964 there were fewer than 10 journalists in Vietnam, but by 1968 there were over 600. Television also played a part in bringing the war into American homes.

What are some examples of media coverage of the Vietnam War?

Examples of media coverage of the Vietnam War *(p.91)* included:

- The Tet Offensive in January 1968. Coverage showed Vietnamese civilians being killed and ancient monuments destroyed.
- In February 1968 there were news stories of General Nguyen Ngoc Loan's execution of a Vietcong fighter.
- In November 1969 the media broke the truth about the My Lai Massacre.

Why was there an increase in media coverage of the Vietnam War?

Media coverage of the Vietnam War *(p.91)* increased for the following reasons:

- To begin with, there were few troops in Vietnam. In 1960 there were only 900 'military advisers', and no reporters.
- This changed in 1960 when local Vietnamese people were killed in an attack against Diem, the South Vietnamese president. Many journalists travelled to Vietnam to report on the event.
- As US involvement in the war increased, so too did the number of journalists covering the conflict. By 1965 there were 400 foreign news reporters in Vietnam - an increase of 900 per cent on 1964.
- Since the Second World War, there had been a significant increase in the number of Americans who owned a television. In 1948, just 1 per cent of American households had a television; by 1961, this had risen to 93 per cent.

- Journalists were better equipped to report the news with ground-breaking technology such as video cameras and voice recorders. It helped reporters capture the reality of the war and broadcast it to America and the world.
- There was no censorship on coverage of the Vietnam War (p.91). The Second World War and Korean War (p.26) had been filmed by military cameramen, but Vietnam was caught on film by by independent television networks.

What was the early media coverage of the Vietnam War like?

Early coverage of events in Vietnam mostly included positive reporting on the courage of American soldiers and the new technology used in weaponry. In the context of the Cold War (p.18), it portrayed the USA as the 'goodies', fighting the communist 'baddies' of North Vietnam.

How was the anti-Vietnam War movement portrayed on television?

The media showed the anti-war movement and created momentum for it through television, music, and key public figures.

How did television portray the civil rights movement's views on the Vietnam War?

Civil rights activists such as Martin Luther King, Muhammad Ali, and the Black Panthers (p.73) were among those who spoke out. They opposed black people having to fight for America when they faced racism at home.

How was music used in coverage of the anti-Vietnam War movement on television?

Music was a massive medium for the anti-war movement to express its beliefs. Music from Bob Dylan, John Lennon and Jimi Hendrix among others helped create a young generation that opposed the war.

What were the 'five o'clock follies' in media coverage of the Vietnam War?

As the war intensified in the mid 1960s, US forces met with journalists covering the conflict daily at 5:00pm. The journalists would jeer and mock the military officials as they felt the truth was being hidden about the extent of failures of the US Army in Vietnam. These meetings became known as the 'five o'clock follies' as they were seen as useless.

What was the significance of media coverage of the Tet Offensive in the Vietnam War?

The TV media coverage of the Tet Offensive was significant for the following reasons:
- The coverage resulted in a change in how the war was reported and how the public perceived the conflict.
- For many months officials had assured the public that they were winning the war, however the TV media coverage of the Tet Offensive contradicted this.
- TV reports of the Tet Offensive showed the fall of the US embassy of Saigon - a symbolic defeat in the eyes of Americans (although the US eventually won it back).
- Viewers saw the brutality of the war, and after the Tet Offensive many people did not trust what they were being told.

How did media coverage expose the government's lies to the public about the Vietnam War?

People lost faith when they realised the government was not being completely honest about what was happening in Vietnam. For example, the US government (p.16) claimed victory in the Tet Offensive, but CBS journalist Walter Cronkite reported the reality and showed that it was a stalemate.

What role did television play in the anti-war movement and Vietnam?

Television played a part in affecting public opinion. It showed the civil rights movement, music, Watergate (p.103) and the Pentagon Papers, as well as live broadcasts from Vietnam.

What was the 'credibility gap' on television during the Vietnam War?

The 'credibility gap' was the term used to describe the difference between what the US government (p.16) said was happening, and what people saw happening on TV.

What was the significance of Walter Cronkite's role in media coverage of the Vietnam War?

The role of Walter Cronkite was significant for the following reasons:

- Walter Cronkite was a famous news broadcaster, seen as one of the 'most trusted men in America'. His coverage of the war played a huge role in the peace movement.
- In one of his news broadcasts for CBS, in February 1967, he said: 'It seems now more certain than ever, that the bloody experience of Vietnam is to end a stalemate... it is increasingly clear to the only rational way out then will be to negotiate.'.
- Cronkite was so influential that President Johnson *(p.82)* once said to an advisor: 'If I have lost Cronkite, I've lost this country.'.
- When Walter Cronkite made his famous statement on the Tet Offensive in 1968, it was considered a turning point in the media and public attitude, and the beginning of the fading of support for the war.

What was the significance of media coverage of the My Lai Massacre in the Vietnam War?

Coverage of the My Lai Massacre in March 1968, was significant because it damaged the reputation of the US forces. Americans were shocked and appalled about both the reports of their soldiers murdering innocent people but also the fact that the army and government had tried to cover it up.

What was the impact of media coverage of the Vietnam War?

The TV media coverage of the Vietnam War *(p.91)* had the following impacts:

- It led to a lack of trust in the US Army and the government. When the New York Times published leaked reports of American actions in Vietnam in June 1971 that were supposed to be secret many felt they had been lied to about the war.
- The media coverage influenced public opinion. When the names and faces of over 200 US soldiers were published during a week of fighting in 1969, people became angry about fighting a distant war.
- As more and more stories were published of soldiers and civilians dying and the brutality of the war, this affected the morale and behaviour in the US forces.
- The failure of US tactics in Vietnam was widely published and clear for Americans to see on the television and this led to more people questioning the point of the war and if the USA could win.
- The anti-war movement was further strengthened by the TV media coverage of the conflict.

DID YOU KNOW?

'Television brought the brutality of war into the comfort of the living room. Vietnam was lost in the living rooms of America - not on the battlefields of Vietnam.' - Marshall McLuhan

Vietnam was known as the 'first television war'.

WOMEN'S MOVEMENT

'Human rights are women's rights, and women's rights are human rights.' - Hillary Clinton

What was the 1960s American women's movement?

Inspired by the civil rights movement, women began to campaign for equal rights during the 1960s.

What was the attitude to women in America in the 1960s?

The 2 main traditional views of a woman's role in the 1960s were:

- A woman's place was in the home, looking after the children.
- Once married, a woman was expected to give up her job and become a housewife.

Why did women start protesting in America in the 1960s?

There were 6 main reasons women began to protest during the 1960s:

- Eleanor Roosevelt *(p.97)*, the wife of President Roosevelt, had campaigned for women's rights since the 1930s and this encouraged women to protest.
- Betty Friedan's *(p.98)* book, 'The Feminine Mystique', explored the position and role of women and raised the case for equality, influencing many women.
- Women were unhappy they did not receive equal pay to men for doing the same job, as discovered by the Presidential Commission on the Status of Women.
- The 1960s was a period of protest and the civil rights movement influenced many women.
- The increased desire for gadgets like the television and labour-saving devices such as the washing machine meant households needed more than one wage-earner to afford them. Such devices also meant women had more time and so could work outside the home.
- The development of the contraceptive pill from 1960 meant women could choose when they had a family and plan their career and education around it.

Who influenced the women's movement in America in the 1960s?

There were 5 main groups and individuals influential in the women's movement:

- Eleanor Roosevelt *(p.97)*, the wife of President Roosevelt.
- Betty Friedan *(p.98)*, author of 'The Feminine Mystique'.
- The National Organisation of Women, or NOW.
- Stop Taking Our Privileges (STOP) by Phyllis Schlafly *(p.99)*.
- The Women's Liberation Movement *(p.101)*.

Why did some people not agree with the women's movement in America in the 1960s?

There were 3 key reasons people opposed the women's movement:

- Some people objected to equality, believing in traditional gender roles. They thought the women's movement was damaging to society and family life.
- Those who strongly opposed the women's movement said all feminists were lesbians.
- There was opposition to some of the movement's aims, particularly its demands on abortion *(p.102)*, which drove many women to form and join other groups that supported a woman's traditional role as homemaker.

How did some people oppose the women's movement in the 1960s?

There were 3 ways in which people opposed the women's movement:

- The women's movement attracted a lot of negative publicity and media coverage was often negative.
- Those who took part in protests were often verbally abused and sometimes attacked.
- Groups such as Stop Taking Our Privileges (STOP) by Phyllis Schlafly *(p.99)* were set up by those who opposed certain aims of the women's movement.

Was the women's movement a success in America in the 1960s?

There were 6 main achievements:

- Equal pay for men and women who were doing the same job was made law in the Equal Pay Act of 1963.

- NOW, or the National Organisation of Women, won several court cases in which women who were paid less than men for doing the same job were awarded money.
- Discrimination based on gender was made illegal in the Civil Rights Act of 1964.
- Sex discrimination in education was made illegal in the Education Amendment Act of 1972, which stated boys and girls should follow the same school curriculum.
- The women's movement led to the legalisation of abortion *(p.102)* through the Roe v. Wade *(p.102)* court case in 1973.
- More women were encouraged to become politically active and work in a wider range of jobs. The traditional role of women was challenged.

What were the limitations of the women's movement in America in the 1960s?

There were 3 main limitations to the achievements of the women's movement:

- The number of women in management roles remained very low.
- Sexism still existed.
- Equal pay is still an issue today.

> **DID YOU KNOW?**
>
> One famous women's rights protest was organised for the 1968 Miss America competition.
>
> The Women's Liberation Movement protested by crowning a sheep 'Miss America' and held signs showing women being treated like cattle.

ELEANOR ROOSEVELT

'We must know what we think and speak out, even at the risk of unpopularity.' - Eleanor Roosevelt, 1963

Who was Eleanor Roosevelt?

Eleanor Roosevelt was the wife of the 32nd President of the USA, Franklin D Roosevelt. She played an important role in campaigning for women's rights.

When did Eleanor Roosevelt campaign for women's rights?

Eleanor Roosevelt campaigned for women's rights between 1933 and 1962.

How did Eleanor Roosevelt campaign for women?

Eleanor Roosevelt took 4 key actions:

- She held press conferences and only allowed women to attend, ensuring media outlets had to employ female journalists.
- She put pressure on her husband and other politicians to employ more women.
- She made radio and television broadcasts and wrote articles sharing her opinions on many issues, including women's rights.
- She agreed to support John F Kennedy's *(p.80)* campaign to become president if he agreed to look into the status of women through the creation of a commission.

How did Eleanor Roosevelt help women?

Eleanor Roosevelt achieved 3 key successes:

- The President's Commission on the Status of Women, created in 1961, highlighted inequality for women in the workplace in terms of pay and opportunity.
- Two laws were passed in the 1960s partly as a result of the Commission's findings. The Equal Pay Act in June 1963 made it illegal to pay people differently for the same job, while the Civil Rights Act of 1964 made it illegal to discriminate against someone based on gender.
- She was internationally respected and helped write the United Nations' Universal Declaration of Human Rights, which is still in existence today.

> **DID YOU KNOW?**
>
> **President Truman had hinted he would be willing to make Eleanor Roosevelt his vice-presidential candidate.**
>
> However, she did not want to be elected to a political position.

BETTY FRIEDAN

'Who knows what women can be when they are finally free to become themselves?' - Betty Friedan, The Feminine Mystique

Who was Betty Friedan?

Betty Friedan was a journalist and a leading figure in the women's movement during the 1960s. She wrote 'The Feminine Mystique' and co-founded the National Organisation for Women.

What did Betty Friedan's book say?

In her book 'The Feminine Mystique', published in 1963, Friedan said women should have equal rights with men in every way and that women should be able to pursue a good career.

How important was Betty Friedan?

Her book became a bestseller and was very influential in changing thinking about women's roles.

> **DID YOU KNOW?**
>
> **Friedan's 'The Feminine Mystique' was fuelled by a high school reunion.**
>
> At the reunion, Friedan discovered most of her classmates were unsatisfied with their limited roles as suburban housewives.

PHYLLIS SCHLAFLY

'Women have babies and men provide the support. If you don't like the way we're made you've got to take it up with God.' - Phyllis Schlafly

Who was Phyllis Schlafly?

Phyllis Schlafly was an anti-feminist campaigner who believed strongly in the traditional role of women.

How did Schlafly oppose the women's movement?

Phyllis Schlafly took 3 main actions:

- She created the Eagle Forum, a conservative organisation that was pro-life and anti-abortion, in 1967.
- She made speeches and wrote articles convincing many women to join the anti-feminist cause.
- Schlafly campaigned throughout the USA. In 1972 the Eagle Forum became STOP, or Stop Taking Our Privileges, an organisation that aimed to prevent the Equal Rights Amendment *(p.101)* being ratified by states.

DID YOU KNOW?

Despite arguing against feminism, Schlafly was a powerful woman.

She was frequently a delegate at Republican national conventions, had her own newspaper column and a weekly radio show, and wrote and edited 27 books.

EQUAL PAY ACT, 1963

'We sought justice because equal pay for equal work is an American value.' - Lilly Ledbetter

What was the campaign for equal pay?

The campaign for equal pay resulted in the Equal Pay Act of 1963.

Why did the campaign for equal pay start?

Women's groups began to campaign for equal pay as, by 1960, women still earned less than two-thirds than their male counterparts.

Who supported the campaign for equal pay?

The campaign was supported by former First Lady Eleanor Roosevelt *(p.97)* and the head of the Women's Bureau of the Department of Labour, Esther Peterson.

Who opposed the campaign for equal pay?

There was opposition from powerful business groups such as the Chamber of Commerce, as well as from many Republican politicians.

> **DID YOU KNOW?**
>
> **The Equal Pay Act 1963 stated:**
> 'No employer ...shall discriminate ...between employees on the basis of sex.'

NATIONAL ORGANISATION FOR WOMEN

'The time has come for a new movement toward true equality for all women in America.' - National Organisation for Women

What was the National Organisation for Women?
The National Organisation for Women, or NOW, was created to attract supporters and put pressure on the government to enforce equality. Betty Friedan *(p.98)* was its first president.

When was the National Organisation for Women set up?
The National Organisation for Women, or NOW, was created in 1966.

Why was the National Organisation for Women set up?
The National Organisation for Women was set up for 2 main reasons:
- ✅ The Equal Pay Act of 1963 had not solved the problem of unequal pay for women and men for doing the same job. Women were still being paid less than men.
- ✅ Existing protest movements for civil rights and students were not tackling the issues of sexism.

What were the National Organisation for Women's aims?
NOW demanded equal rights for women in US law, as well as the right of women to choose when they had children.

How many members did the National Organisation for Women have?
By the end of the 1960s, NOW had around 40,000 members.

How did the National Organisation for Women campaign?
They used a variety of tactics and methods to try and bring about change, including protest marches, petitions and strikes.

What impact did the National Organisation for Women have?
The National Organisation for Women achieved 2 main successes:
- ✅ NOW increased awareness of the inequality faced by women and inspired many to challenge the system.
- ✅ The organisation successfully fought a number of court cases and won compensation for women from businesses that failed to pay them the same wage as men, despite the Equal Pay Act of 1963.

What were the main failures of the National Organisation for Women?
There were 2 main ways in which NOW failed:

- ☑ Some considered NOW too radical, particularly on its support for abortion *(p.102)* and the Equal Rights Amendment *(p.101)*.
- ☑ Many felt NOW did not do enough to help poorer women as the majority of its members tended to be middle or upper class.

> **DID YOU KNOW?**
>
> As of 2020, NOW was still the largest feminist group in the USA, with more than half a million members.

EQUAL RIGHTS AMENDMENT, 1972

'My greatest disappointment in all the projects I worked on during the White House years was the failure of the Equal Rights Amendment to be ratified.' - Rosalynn Carter

What was the Equal Rights Amendment?

The Equal Rights Amendment was - and still is - a proposed amendment to the United States Constitution to guarantee women will be treated equally to men.

Why was the Equal Rights Amendment not ratified?

There were 2 main reasons why the ERA was not ratified:

- ☑ The Equal Rights Amendment was presented to Congress repeatedly from 1923. It was eventually passed in 1972, but then had to be ratified by individual states.
- ☑ Phyllis Schlafly's *(p.99)* Stop ERA campaign delayed the ratification of the Equal Rights Amendment. By 1982 - the deadline for ratification - only 35 of the required 38 states had agreed.

When was the Equal Rights Amendment eventually passed?

In 2020, the ERA was still not law in the US.

> **DID YOU KNOW?**
>
> **There has been a campaign for an Equal Rights Amendment for almost 100 years.**
>
> The first was introduced in Congress in 1923.

WOMEN'S LIBERATION MOVEMENT

'I'm a feminist. I've been female for a long time now. It'd be stupid not to be on my own side.' - Maya Angelou

What was the Women's Liberation Movement?

The Women's Liberation Movement was the name given to a group of women whose aims were more radical. They wanted to destroy the existing system and free women from a male-dominated society.

How did the Women's Liberation Movement protest?

The Women's Liberation Movement's tactics changed over time:

- ✓ At first their protests were aggressive. As an example, at the 1968 Miss America contest they threw bras, makeup and other products they felt proved society only valued women for their looks into bins.
- ✓ Following a lot of negative publicity they changed their approach. They began to help at a local level by creating discussion groups for women to talk about their experiences in work and education.
- ✓ By the mid-1970s, they were also helping women to deal with issues such as domestic violence and rape.

> **DID YOU KNOW?**
> Feminism is often seen as coming in 'waves'. The period from 1963 to the 1980s is known as the second wave.

ABORTION

'It is simply the right to choose, which is an essential value.' - Betty Friedan

What were the views on abortion in America in the 1960s?

In 1960, abortion was illegal in the USA unless the mother's life was at risk.

What changes did states make to abortion law in America after the 1960s?

Some states changed their laws to allow abortion in certain circumstances, such as if the pregnancy was the result of a rape. In 1970, New York changed its law to allow abortion up to the 24th week of pregnancy.

What was the legal ruling that changed the law on abortion in America after the 1960s?

Roe v Wade *(p. 102)* was a landmark ruling in January 1973 that established a woman's legal right to abortion. The case led to abortions becoming more widely available to women throughout the USA.

> **DID YOU KNOW?**
> It is estimated around 35% of all American women will have had an abortion by the time they are 45 years old.

ROE V WADE, 1973

'I long for the day that Roe v Wade is sent to the ash heap of history.' - Vice-President Mike Pence

What was Roe v Wade?

Roe v Wade was a case before the Supreme Court, where lawyers successfully argued that a 21-year-old woman had the right to an abortion *(p. 102)*. The Supreme Court ruled all women had the right to safe and legal abortions.

Who was opposed to Roe v Wade?

There was, and continues to be, huge opposition to Roe v Wade. The 2 main forms are:

- Many states which had previously banned abortion *(p.102)* tried to make it very difficult for women to have access to the procedure.
- The National Right to Life Committee formed with the goal of reversing the Roe v Wade decision.

> **DID YOU KNOW?**
>
> **McCorvey (Roe), the Texas resident who wanted an abortion, changed sides on the abortion debate and campaigned for abortion to be outlawed.**
>
> Since her death in 2017 it has been revealed anti-abortion campaigners paid her to do so.

WATERGATE SCANDAL, 1972

'It was accountability that Nixon feared.' - Bob Woodward, journalist

What was Watergate?

Watergate was a political scandal involving President Richard Nixon, leading to his resignation in 1974.

When did the Watergate scandal happen?

The events of Watergate took place between 1971 and 1974. The burglary at the centre of the scandal happened on 17th June, 1972. Details were first published in the media during that month, and eventually it led to Nixon's resignation on 9th August, 1974.

Who was involved with the Watergate scandal?

There were 4 main individuals or groups involved in Watergate:

- President Richard Nixon, who lied about interfering with the investigation.
- The Committee to Re-elect the President, or CREEP.
- Washington Post journalists Carl Bernstein and Bob Woodward, who investigated the events.
- The FBI, who investigated what happened.

How was Nixon involved in Watergate?

President Richard Nixon was involved in the Watergate scandal in 5 main ways:

- CREEP, or the Committee to Re-elect the President, was created to raise money for his 1972 re-election campaign. It committed crimes by spying on his opponents, the Democrats.
- He provided funds for CREEP that enabled its members to spy. Some of the money was used to fund a break-in at the National Democratic Committee offices.
- He blocked the initial investigation, attempted to cover up the wrongdoing, and interfered with the FBI's investigation.
- He initially refused to hand over tapes of conversations held in the Oval Office to the FBI which contained evidence relevant to their investigation.
- He resigned as president on 9th August, 1974, before he could be impeached for his involvement in the scandal.

Who were the White House Plumbers in the Watergate scandal?

The White House Plumbers was a group created by President Nixon to prevent sensitive information being leaked.

What did CREEP do in the Watergate scandal?

There are 3 main facts to note about CREEP:

- ✅ CREEP, or the Committee to Re-elect the President, was created to raise money for Nixon's 1972 re-election campaign.
- ✅ John Mitchell, a former attorney general, was made director of the committee. Nixon had secretly provided Mitchell with a fund to pay the White House Plumbers to spy on and damage his opponents.
- ✅ CREEP successfully disgraced a number of potential Democratic candidates.

What happened at the Watergate complex?

Five men were arrested while breaking into the National Democratic Committee offices on the Watergate complex in Washington DC on 17th June, 1972. They were caught trying to repair bugging devices.

Who were the Washington Post reporters investigating the Watergate scandal?

The Washington Post played 3 main roles in the Watergate scandal:

- ✅ Two reporters, Bob Woodward and Carl Bernstein, investigated the break-in and found connections to CREEP.
- ✅ John Mitchell denied any link between CREEP and the burglary, but the reporters continued investigating.
- ✅ They played a key role in bringing Watergate to the public's attention and also persuading the Democrats that investigation of the issue was needed.

What did the FBI investigation into the Watergate scandal find?

The FBI played 3 main roles in Watergate:

- ✅ Sources inside the FBI provided evidence to Woodward and Bernstein, showing the break-in was linked to CREEP.
- ✅ The FBI also carried out its own investigation and discovered links between two of the White House Plumbers (who had planned the break-in) and CREEP.
- ✅ Over the next two years the FBI uncovered the extent of the campaign to spy on and damage the Democrats, and found it had been financed by CREEP.

What was the Watergate scandal?

There were 5 main reasons Watergate was a scandal:

- ✅ At first, most people did not believe government officials would be involved in illegal activity, especially when President Nixon publicly stated that White House lawyer John Dean had investigated and found no links to anyone inside.
- ✅ In January 1973, the trial of the five burglars and two White House Plumbers began. Two of the defendants were found guilty and five pleaded guilty. Before sentencing, the judge received a letter from one of the burglars claiming White House officials had told them to lie during the trial.
- ✅ Nixon denied involvement and ordered an investigation led by a special prosecutor. After this, the White House announced both Chiefs of Staff had been sacked and the head of the White House Plumbers had resigned for their involvement in the burglary and subsequent cover-up.
- ✅ At the same time, the Senate set up the Select Committee on Presidential Campaign Activities to investigate. Their meetings were televised across the US.
- ✅ The nation was particularly shocked by testimony from one of the fired White House Chiefs of Staff, which suggested Nixon had been involved.

What did the Watergate recordings reveal?

The White House recordings revealed 5 main issues:

- All conversations and phone calls in President Nixon's office were recorded. The investigation's special prosecutor and the select committee demanded access to the recordings but Nixon refused every time, saying to release them would be a national security concern.
- In October 1973 Nixon eventually released some edited scripts. More followed in April 1974, unedited but with bad language removed and replaced with the words 'expletive deleted'.
- Nixon's reluctance to allow access to the actual recordings, and the fact some scripts had been edited, led the Senate to consider impeaching Nixon.
- Nixon eventually released the recordings, which revealed the extent of his involvement. This included blocking the initial investigation, abusing his power and failing to follow the law.
- A recording from 23rd June, 1972, revealed Nixon had tried to prevent the FBI investigating the break-in and proved he was involved from the beginning.

Who became president after Nixon resigned over Watergate?

Gerald Ford was the 38th US president, holding the office from 1974-77. He was sworn in as president following Richard Nixon's resignation.

Why did Ford pardon Nixon for Watergate?

Nixon was pardoned by Gerald Ford for any crimes he may have committed. Ford said it was the only way America could move on from Watergate.

What were the consequences of Watergate?

Watergate impacted both Nixon and US politics in 6 key ways:

- It ended Richard Nixon's political career. Although he resigned stating it was for the good of the country, in reality he had no choice as he would likely have been impeached. It also destroyed his reputation.
- The White House recordings showed the public how the president's office behaved. Many were shocked at how the president spoke about others and the bad language used.
- Many government officials were sent to prison, resulting in a big change in government staff.
- The next presidential election saw Jimmy Carter, a Democrat, become president. He was honest, religious and well-liked, but lacked the skills needed to be a strong leader.
- Many Americans lost trust in the government and fewer people voted or wanted to become politicians.
- A series of laws were passed to prevent Watergate happening again and stop presidents acting without the approval of Congress.

What laws were introduced because of the Watergate scandal?

There were 5 main laws introduced because of the Watergate scandal:

- The War Powers Act of 1973 meant the president could not go to war without the support of Congress.
- The Elections Campaigning Act of 1974 set limits to the size of the contributions that could be made for elections and how much political parties could spend.
- The Congressional Budget Control Act of 1974 meant the president could not use government money for personal use.
- The Freedom of Information Act of 1974 meant people had the right to access documents held on them by the federal government.
- The Privacy Act of 1974 stated the rules government had to follow when collecting people's private data.

What was the impact of the Watergate scandal on the Vietnam War?

The scandal hugely eroded the public's trust in American politics and people began to wonder how many cover-ups there were in the Vietnam War *(p.91)*. People simply did not trust what they were being told and the anti-war movement was further strengthened.

> **DID YOU KNOW?**
>
> **Lots of scandals now have the suffix -gate as a result of the Watergate scandal.**
>
> The name Watergate originally comes from the complex of six buildings in Washington DC where the burglary of the Democratic National Committee took place.

GLOSSARY

A

Abolish, Abolished - to stop something, or get rid of it.

Aggression - angry, hostile or violent behaviour displayed without provocation.

Agricultural - relating to agriculture.

Alliance - a union between groups or countries that benefits each member.

Allies - parties working together for a common objective, such as countries involved in a war. In both world wars, 'Allies' refers to those countries on the side of Great Britain.

Amputate, Amputation - to surgically remove a limb from someone's body.

Armistice - an agreement between two or more opposing sides in a war to stop fighting.

Artillery - large guns used in warfare.

Assassinate - to murder someone, usually an important figure, often for religious or political reasons.

Assassination - the act of murdering someone, usually an important person.

Attorney general - the main legal advisor to the government.

B

Blacklist - the blocking of trade as a means to punish.

Blockade - a way of blocking or sealing an area to prevent goods, supplies or people from entering or leaving. It often refers to blocking transport routes.

Boycott - a way of protesting or bringing about change by refusing to buy something or use services.

Bribe, Bribery, Bribes - to dishonestly persuade someone to do something for you in return for money or other inducements.

Buffer - a protective barrier.

Buffer zone - a neutral area of land to separate hostile forces or nations and provide protection. In the Cold War, Eastern Europe was the buffer zone between Western Europe and the USSR.

C

Campaign - a political movement to get something changed; in military terms, it refers to a series of operations to achieve a goal.

Capitalism - the idea of goods and services being exchanged for money, private ownership of property and businesses, and acceptance of a hierarchical society.

Censorship - the control of information in the media by a government, whereby information considered obscene or unacceptable is suppressed.

Civil rights - the rights a citizen has to political or social freedoms, such as the right to vote or freedom of speech.

Civilian - a non-military person.

Claim - someone's assertion of their right to something - for example, a claim to the throne.

Coalition government - a government formed by more than one political party.

Coalition, Coalitions - a temporary alliance, such as when a group of countries fights together.

Commune - a place where a group of people live and work together and share resources.

Communism - the belief, based on the ideas of Karl Marx, that all people should be equal in society without government, money or private property. Everything is owned by by the people, and each person receives according to need.

Communist - a believer in communism.

Conference - a formal meeting to discuss common issues of interest or concern.

Conservative - someone who dislikes change and prefers traditional values. It can also refer to a member of the Conservative Party.

Constitution - rules, laws or principles that set out how a country is governed.

Constitutional - relating to the constitution.

Containment - meaning to keep something under control or within limits, it often refers to the American idea of stopping the spread of communism.

Corrupt - when someone is willing to act dishonestly for their own personal gain.

Council - an advisory or administrative body set up to manage the affairs of a place or organisation. The Council of the League of Nations contained the organisation's most powerful members.

Crusades - a series of religious wars during the Middle Ages where the Christians of Europe tried to take control of the holy land (Jerusalem).

Culture - the ideas, customs, and social behaviour of a particular people or society.

Currency - an umbrella term for any form of legal tender, but most commonly referring to money.

D

Deadlock - a situation where no action can be taken and neither side can make progress against the other; effectively a draw.

Democracy - a political system where a population votes for its government on a regular basis. The word is Greek for 'the rule of people' or 'people power'.

Democratic - relating to or supporting the principles of democracy.

Deploy - to move military troops or equipment into position or a place so they are ready for action.

Desegregation - a policy of removing racial segregation (separation).

GLOSSARY

Discriminate, Discrimination - to treat a person or group of people differently and in an unfair way.

Dispute - a disagreement or argument; often used to describe conflict between different countries.

Dissolution, Dissolve - the formal ending of a partnership, organisation or official body.

Doctrine - a stated principle of government policy; can also refer to a set of beliefs held and taught by a church, political party or other group.

Dollar imperialism - a phrase used by the Soviet Union's Foreign Minister, Molotov, in accusing the USA of using its economic strength to take over Europe through the Marshall Plan.

E

Economic - relating to the economy; also used when justifying something in terms of profitability.

Economy - a country, state or region's position in terms of production and consumption of goods and services, and the supply of money.

Embassy - historically, a deputation sent by one ruler, state or country to another. More recently, it is also the accepted name for the official residence or offices of an ambassador.

Exile - to be banned from one's original country, usually as a punishment or for political reasons.

Extreme - furthest from the centre or any given point. If someone holds extreme views, they are not moderate and are considered radical.

F

Fascist - one who believes in fascism.

Federal - in US politics this means 'national', referring to the whole country rather than any individual state.

Feminist - someone who believes in feminism.

Figurehead - Someone who acts as a symbolic leader for something.

Foreign policy - a government's strategy for dealing with other nations.

Free elections - elections in which voters are free to vote without interference.

Full employment - when virtually everyone able and willing to work in a country has a job.

G

Ghetto - part of a city, often a slum area, occupied by a minority group.

Guerrilla tactics, Guerrilla warfare - a way of fighting that typically involves hit-and-run style tactics.

H

Hippies - Groups of Americans who 'dropped out' of traditional life. Most did not go to college or work and travelled around the country, organising music festivals and protests against the Vietnam war and campaigning for world peace.

I

Ideology - a set of ideas and ideals, particularly around political ideas or economic policy, often shared by a group of people.

Immigrant - someone who moves to another country.

Immigration - the act of coming to a foreign country with the intention of living there permanently.

Impeach, Impeachment - to charge someone, usually a high-ranking government official, with treason or a crime against the state.

Imperial, Imperialisation, Imperialism, Imperialist - is the practice or policy of taking possession of, and extending political and economic control over other areas or territories. Imperialism always requires the use of military, political or economic power by a stronger nation over that of a weaker one. An imperialist is someone who supports or practices imperialism and imperial relates to a system of empire, for example the British Empire.

Independence, Independent - to be free of control, often meaning by another country, allowing the people of a nation the ability to govern themselves.

Industry - the part of the economy concerned with turning raw materials into into manufactured goods, for example making furniture from wood.

Inferior - lower in rank, status or quality.

Integrate - to bring people or groups with specific characteristics or needs into equal participation with others; to merge one thing with another to form a single entity.

Intercontinental ballistic missile - a guided ballistic missile with a minimum range of 5,500km or 3,400 miles.

Iron Curtain - a phrase used by Winston Churchill to describe the non-physical divide created by Stalin between Eastern Europe and the West.

J

Juries, Jury - a group of people sworn to listen to evidence on a legal case and then deliver an impartial verdict based on what they have heard.

L

Left wing - used to describe political groups or individuals with beliefs that are usually centered around socialism and the idea of reform.

Legislation - a term for laws when they are considered collectively, for example housing legislation.

Legislature - The organisation or set of people who have the power to create laws.

GLOSSARY

Legitimacy, Legitimate - accepted by law or conforming to the rules; can be defended as valid.

Loophole - an ambiguity or inadequacy in the law or a set of rules which allows people to do something that would otherwise be forbidden or illegal.

Lynch, Lynched, Lynching - the killing of someone by a group of people for an alleged offence without a legal trial, usually publicly and often by hanging.

M

Middle class - refers to the socio-economic group which includes people who are educated and have professional jobs, such as teachers or lawyers.

Militant - using violent or more aggressive methods in a protest or for a cause.

Minister - a senior member of government, usually responsible for a particular area such as education or finance.

Moderate - someone who is not extreme.

Morale - general mood of a group of people.

N

National Guard - A reserve force of the US Army.

Nationalism, Nationalist, Nationalistic - identifying with your own nation and supporting its interests, often to the detriment or exclusion of other nations.

O

Occupation - the action, state or period when somewhere is taken over and occupied by a military force.

P

Peasant - a poor farmer.

Persecute - to treat someone unfairly because of their race, religion or political beliefs.

Pilgrimage - journey undertaken to a sacred place, usually for religious or spiritual reasons.

Poll - a vote or survey.

Polling Station - a place where people go to vote.

Population - the number of people who live in a specified place.

Poverty - the state of being extremely poor.

Precedent - an earlier event used as an example in later, similar situations; often used the courts when they rule on a case similar to one held previously.

Predecessor - the person who came before; the previous person to fill a role or position.

Prejudice - prejudgement - when you assume something about someone based on a feature like their religion or skin colour, rather than knowing it as fact.

President - the elected head of state of a republic.

Prevent, Preventative, Preventive - steps taken to stop something from happening.

Propaganda - biased information aimed at persuading people to think a certain way.

Prosecute - to institute or conduct legal proceedings against a person or organisation.

Provision - the act of providing or supplying something for someone.

Proxy war - a conflict between two sides acting on behalf of other parties who are not directly involved, but who have usually supplied equipment, arms and/or money.

R

Radical, Radicalism - people who want complete or extensive change, usually politically or socially.

Rallies, Rally - a political event with speakers and a crowd, designed to increase support for a politician, political party or an idea.

Ratification, Ratified - to give formal agreement or consent to something.

Rational - when something is based on reason or logic, like science.

Rebels - people who rise in opposition or armed resistance against an established government or leader.

Republic - a state or country run by elected representatives and an elected/nominated president. There is no monarch.

Revolution - the forced overthrow of a government or social system by its own people.

Rig, Rigged - politically, to interfere in or fix an election to determine the winner.

Riots - violent disturbances involving a crowd of people.

S

Satellite state - a country under the control of another, such as countries under USSR control during the Cold War.

Scandal, Scandalous - something that angers or shocks people because rules or accepted standards of behaviour have been broken.

Segregation - when people are kept separately from each other - often used in the context of race.

Soviet - an elected workers' council at local, regional or national level in the former Soviet Union. It can also be a reference to the Soviet Union or the USSR.

Stalemate - a situation where no action can be taken and neither side can make progress against the other; effectively a draw.

State, States - an area of land or a territory ruled by one government.

Strike - a refusal by employees to work as a form of protest, usually to bring about change in their working conditions. It puts pressure on their employer, who cannot run the business without workers.

T

Tactic - a strategy or method of achieving a goal.

Territories, Territory - an area of land under the control of a ruler/country.

Trade unions - organised groups of workers who cooperate to make their lives better at work. For example, they might negotiate for better pay and then organise a strike if one is refused.

Treason - the crime of betraying one's country, often involving an attempt to overthrow the government or kill the monarch.

Treaty - a formal agreement, signed and ratified by two or more parties.

U

Unconstitutional - not in accordance with the constitution of a country or organisation.

Upper class - a socio-economic group consisting of the richest people in a society who are wealthy because they own land or property.

V

Veto - the right to reject a decision or proposal.

W

WASP - white Anglo-Saxon Protestant.

Welfare - wellbeing; often refers to money and services given to the poorest people.

Western powers - a group term used to describe developed capitalist nations, such as Britain and the USA.

White supremacist - one who believes white people are superior to people of other ethnicities and should therefore be dominant.

INDEX

A
Abortion - *102*
African American life, 1950s - *35*
Arms Race - *26*
Assassination of Martin Luther King - *78*

B
Berkeley - *88*
Berlin Airlift - *25*
Berlin Blockade - *24*
Black Panthers - *73*
Black Power movement - *70*
Brown v Topeka - *43*
Bussing - *50*

C
CORE - *40*
Campaign C - *59*
Campaign for Equal Pay - *99*
Carmichael, Stokely - *72*
Churches support of Civil Rights Movement - *42*
Civil Rights Act 1957 - *51*
Civil Rights Act 1964 - *65*
Civil Rights Act 1968 - *79*
Civil Rights and Nixon - *83*
Civil Rights organisations - *39*
Cold War - *18*
Congress of Racial Equality - *40*

D
Discrimination in the USA - *37*
Dixiecrats - *54*

E
Equal Rights Amendment - *101*

F
Freedom Riders - *57*
Freedom Summer - *62*
Friedan, Betty - *98*

G
Government, US system - *16*

Greensboro Sit-in - *55*
Growth of Protests - *84*

H
Hippies - *90*
Hiss, Alger - *32*
Hollywood Ten - *31*

I
Iron Curtain Speech - *21*

J
James Meredith Case - *59*
Johnson, Lyndon B - *82*

K
Kennedy's domestic policies - *81*
Kennedy, President - *80*
Kent State Protest - *89*
Kerner Report - *76*
King, Martin Luther - *52*
Korean War - *26*
Ku Klux Klan - *53*

L
Little Rock High School - *48*
Little, Malcolm - *68*

M
Malcolm X - *68*
March on Washington - *61*
Marshall Plan - *23*
Martin Luther King
   Assassination - *78*
   Campaign - *76*
McCarthy, Joseph - *34*
Media war, Vietnam - *93*
Mexico Olympics - *72*
Mississipi Summer Project - *62*
Mississippi Murders - *64*
Montgomery Bus Boycott - *46*

N
NAACP - *39*

INDEX

National Organisation for Women - *100*

O

Opposition to the Civil Rights Movement - *53*

P

Poor People's Campaign - *79*
President Johnson - *82*
President Nixon and Civil Rights - *83*

R

RCNL - *41*
Red Scare - *29*
Regional Council of Negro Leadership - *41*
Riots of 1964 and 1967 - *74*
Roe v Wade - *102*
Roosevelt, Eleanor - *97*
Rosenberg, Ethel and Julius - *33*

S

SCLC - *41*
SNCC - *56*
Schlafly, Phyllis - *99*
Second Red Scare - *29*
Segregation in the USA - *36*
Selma March - *66*
Southern Christian Leadership Council - *41*
Soviet Satellite States - *20*
Student Movement - *86*
Student Nonviolent Coordinating Committee - *56*
Student protest, 1960s - *85*
Support for Black Power - *71*

T

TV during Vietnam War - *93*
Till, Emmett - *44*
Truman Doctrine - *22*
Truman, Harry - *38*

U

US Political system - *18*
US system of government - *16*
University support of the Civil Rights Movement - *42*

V

Vietnam
    The media war - *93*
Vietnam War - *91*
Voting Rights Act - *67*

W

Washington March - *61*
Watergate - *103*
Women in 1960s - *95*
Women's Liberation Movement - *101*